Hilary's Heart

Linda Finnegan

www.pebbleinapondmedia.com

ISBN 978-0-615-23293-5

Printed in the United States of America

First Edition

Pebble in a Pond Media, Culver City, CA
www.pebbleinapondmedia.com

This book is dedicated to the thousands of children around the world who have enriched my life, touched my heart and given more to me than words could ever express.

Contents

Introduction

When trying to decide what I could possibly give to Hilary Duff for her 21st birthday, I thought of many things — none of which seemed quite right. It was while thinking about her unique qualities, her passion and persistence, her drive and desire, her energy and enthusiasm, her care and compassion that I finally realized I should be writing a book about the heartfelt memories I have of—*HER*.

There were many reasons why I wanted to write about her exceptional characteristics, but most importantly, to reveal her caring heart. It was important to me to create something that would be everlasting and would inspire others. I wanted people to learn about her remarkable, and often untold, humanitarian efforts. I wanted to give her something that someday her children and grandchildren could read and discover what her heart was like as a child, a teenager and now, a young adult. I wanted people to know about her acts of kindness and her genuine concern for others. I wanted her philanthropic story to be told and her legacy to continue.

As life goes on, it's interesting to stop every now and then and reflect on our personal journey. To think about where we were in the past, recognize where we are now and anticipate where we want to be in the future can offer valuable insight to who we are today. Reminiscing crucial and pivotal moments in our lives such as tragedies we've endured, challenges we've faced and achievements we've attained, reminds us that these life experiences have all played an important role in our personal growth.

It's easy to think about helping others and being kind to one another although it's not always easy to do, at least not *all* of the time. There are situations throughout our *own* lives when we face challenges and hardships that may seem impossible to understand and create doubt. We may question "Why?" or "Why *me*?" In time, we might recognize these difficulties as important learning experiences that provided us with the opportunity to re-evaluate, re-think and possibly re-direct our focus, emotions, decisions and ultimately our purpose.

Wouldn't it be fascinating if we all knew exactly how our lives would unfold? Even if we did, I'm not sure this knowledge would be beneficial for us. It would most likely change the way we are living today and possibly even prevent us from the enjoyment and the excitement of the many intriguing mysteries and surprises that lie ahead.

When writing *Hilary's Heart* it was my hope that this book would inspire kids and adults everywhere to become more caring and compassionate individuals. I was excited to think that this philanthropic message had the potential to open the hearts of people around the world and encourage them to lend a helping hand to others. I believe that *everyone* can do *something* to make a difference and enhance the life of someone else. It is with thoughtful actions that we promote goodwill and increase opportunities to live in a world that embraces compassion.

Hilary's journey in life, even at the young age of 21, has already exceeded her expectations and fulfilled many of the dreams she had as a child. Her success and fame did not come easy or without sacrifice. She worked hard yet even with an extremely busy schedule, she always made time for others. She learned at a very young age about the importance of lending a helping hand whenever and wherever possible—and these memorable experiences enriched her life in many ways.

By reading this book, if it helps to open *your* heart and encourages you to extend *your* hand to someone in need, I thank you from the bottom of my heart for your desire to make a difference. It is reassuring and comforting to know that the world will be a better place because of your caring heart and actions.

May you be inspired to fulfill your dreams and the dreams of others whose lives you touch.

Chapter 1

We Met In Texas

Hilary Duff as "Wendy"

CASPER meets Wendy

Premiering Only On Video September 22,1998

Hilary signed this photo the first day I met her in Texas. She was only 10½ years old and had just completed *Casper meets Wendy*.

Several years later, Hilary signed the *Casper meets Wendy* DVD for Kids With A Cause to auction. Her signature now looks very different than in earlier years, reflecting a more mature style.

♥

Some people are unforgettable. From the moment you meet them, there is a distinct and lasting impression. Hilary Duff was one of those people to me. She was a cute little blonde ten-year-old with beautiful hazel eyes and a warm and welcoming charm about her that was unique. When I met Hilary, she had just finished filming *Casper meets Wendy* playing the role of *Wendy*. I remember noticing a special sparkle in her eyes but little did I know then what that sparkle was all about. When we were introduced she looked up at me, through her perfectly trimmed bangs, shook my hand and politely smiled. At that time, of course, neither one of us had any idea that we would be spending some remarkable moments together over the next eleven years.

When we met, I was the Executive Director of the Audrey Hepburn Children's Fund. I was creating programs for kids in the entertainment industry to give them opportunities to interact with children in hospitals, group homes, homeless shelters and other youth-based organizations. I realized that these talented young performers had a special place in their hearts for children who were less fortunate. It became very important to me to open the doors of philanthropy by providing enriching experiences that would empower youth. By organizing programs and events that enabled the fortunate and the not-so-fortunate kids to be together, it was my hope that they would share meaningful experiences and make a difference in each other's lives.

Even though I loved creating the programs for the children, I also knew I was running a business and, profit or non-profit, the bills still had to be paid. There were costs involved every time we helped a child. I began to search for potential sponsors in various business sectors. In order to extend our help outside of the Los Angeles area, I decided to seek an airline partner. It was then that I contacted Continental Airlines and learned of their upcoming holiday event—"The North Pole Party."

This annual event was created for terminally ill children who would be spending their holidays in a hospital bed with family members near them. It would not be easy for any of them. In order to bring as much joy as possible to these young patients, the employees of Continental Airlines created and coordinated all of the elements for this magical holiday program that would take place at—the North Pole (well, almost).

The airline volunteers happily donated their time to transform an entire airline hanger to look like the North Pole, only without the snow. There were North Pole signs and decorations, a small train for the children to ride that encircled the perimeter of the huge airline hanger, bounce houses, giant inflatable slides, games, toys, a Texas barbeque, popcorn and cotton candy and Mr. and Mrs. Claus, of course. And to make sure it was extra special there were guest celebrities, both adults and kids, to share in the excitement of this exceptional holiday event.

And who would be attending "The North Pole Party?"—the pediatric patients from MD Anderson and Texas Children's Hospital. These special guests would be accompanied by their parents, siblings and other family relatives, along with the nursing staff and pediatric doctors. I felt privileged that Continental Airlines invited two of our youth celebrities, their parents, and me to fly from Los Angeles to Houston and join in the festivities and the fun.

We arrived safely and were greeted by a group of airline volunteers. We were then taken to our hotel and shortly after we checked in, we attended a brief meeting to discuss the event and find out how we could help. As we heard of the plans, we could hardly wait for the next day when we would meet the children and the fun would begin.

I'll never forget standing at the Continental Airlines gateway in Houston, seeing the young patients and pretending that they were really going on a trip to visit the North Pole. Santa and Mrs. Claus were going on the flight with them and we all waved goodbye as they boarded the two large aircrafts. The parents, nurses, doctors and volunteers also boarded the planes after making sure that the wheelchairs and medical equipment the children needed were safely stored in the cargo compartment.

The young patients fastened their seat belts and up they went on a fantastic ride to the North Pole—Continental-style! As they climbed high in the sky the children sang holiday songs and the planes circled the airport for about fifteen minutes. These young passengers anxiously awaited their arrival to the North Pole—and so did we.

Once the planes were up in the air, the volunteers escorted us to a large van and we drove over to the airline hanger close to where the planes would be landing. We watched as they flew overhead and waited with excitement for their special arrival. While we watched and waited, some of the Continental employees suggested we create a special celebrity welcome for the children.

The celebrities gathered together near the arrival area and began to form two lines facing each other. Hands were joined and held high for the patients to enter "The North Pole" through this unique and exciting passageway. It was while forming this welcome arrival for the patients that Mrs. Duff came up to me because she noticed I was with children. She introduced herself and Hilary and we invited them to join our small group. Hilary seemed pleased to be with others her age since there were a lot more adult athletes than there were child stars. She happily stepped in line with us, clasped hands and had a look of excitement in anticipation of the patients arrival.

When the planes touched down we were ready to welcome the young passengers to "The North Pole" to explore and discover the beautiful winter wonderland created for them. This was one day that, at least for a while, there wouldn't be any reminders of the hospital, the procedures or the pain these young patients faced daily during their short little lives.

The doors opened and the steps came down from each aircraft. Volunteers took their places and began to hand down, from one person to the next, the wheelchairs, the IVs, the oxygen tanks and then the patients. When the children saw everyone and looked at the beautiful holiday decorations, they smiled from ear to ear reflecting their excitement and anticipation of what was ahead.

Everything was fantastic and the kids loved it all. There was a special toy area that Hilary, along with our two young celebrities from Los Angeles, volunteered to work as Santa's helpers. Their "job" was to meet the patients and give gifts to all the children. It was a wonderful day and a time when happiness was clearly visible. What I remember most was seeing smiles and hearing laughter. Yet, I knew that there were some children who were too ill to attend and were still in their hospital beds. My heart ached for them but we had special plans for them, too.

After a few hours of visiting this magical wonderland, it was time for the patients to return to the hospital. They thanked us, hugged us and said goodbye as they boarded the planes with their arms full of gifts and their hearts full of happiness. We stood near the planes and continued to wave long after their seat belts were fastened. We could see how much the trip to "The North Pole" meant to them and knew how grateful they were for this special day.

To help brighten the holidays for those who were unable to attend, I had arranged for a van to take us to the hospitals at the conclusion of "The North Pole Party." We were going to visit the children in their rooms and take them gifts. It was at this time that Mrs. Duff asked me if Hilary could go, too. I'm so glad she asked and joined us because this was the first day that Hilary worked with me and a day that neither one of us will ever forget.

On the way to the hospital, I talked to the kids about the patients we were going to visit and explained why some were unable to attend the holiday celebration. I also discussed the dos and don'ts of interacting with these fragile kids. I reminded them not to ask questions such as, "How long have you been in the hospital?"—or "What's wrong with you?"—or anything about the patients' personal lives. We were not there to discuss their medical situation; we were there to cheer them up, bring them gifts and show them that are people like us who care.

Santa (we actually never asked his real name and always referred to him as *Santa*) rode in the van with us. We decided that in each room Santa would go in first, followed by the celebrity kids and me. Mrs. Duff willingly agreed to stay in the hospital hallways and hand us the gifts to deliver. As we entered each room, there was a special kind of quiet and peacefulness with family members near the child's hospital bed. The nurses who were escorting us always knocked very quietly and asked permission for us to come into the room. Santa led the way and we all followed with our arms loaded with holiday gifts.

In every room, Santa would lean over the bed and ask the young patient if he or she had any special wish for Christmas. In most cases, the answer came in the form of a small shrug followed with, "No, not really." Santa gently continued with "Are you sure there's nothing special I can bring you? I'm right here and you can just whisper your wish to me." There was not one special request—until we met Jasmine.

This young girl, probably only ten or eleven years old, was extremely thin and barely had enough strength to move her small, fragile body. Just as before, Santa asked the same question and got the same reply. When he said to Jasmine, "Are you sure there's not a special wish you have?" she looked up at him and in a very soft voice she replied, "Santa, the only thing I wish is that you could take my pain away."

I felt the lump in my throat and watched the kids hold back their tears as we gave our gifts, extended our holiday wishes and left Jasmine's room. I wasn't sure if the celebrity kids wanted to continue to visit these young patients who may be experiencing their last Christmas. It was difficult to see the kids suffer and to feel so helpless. I took our group out in the hallway to talk with them. I told them that I understood it was not easy and if they preferred, we could leave the gifts with the nurses and they could deliver them for us.

As we sat for a moment to discuss this delicate issue and how, or if, to proceed I saw their eyes filling with tears. Hilary looked up at me with her watery eyes and said, "I *do* want to go to more rooms and see the other kids. I'm okay; it's just that I'm realizing—that could be *me*." She knew, even at her young age, that life is unpredictable and sometimes unfair. She was determined to do all that she could to bring happiness, no matter what it took, to children who were less fortunate.

When we completed all of our patient visits we stood in front of the hospital and the employees of Continental Airlines thanked us for all that we did to bring happiness to the patients. One volunteer, with a camera in her hand, asked if she could take pictures of our group, including Santa and Mrs. Claus, too. There weren't crowds of people around us, we were not being asked to sign autographs and the media wasn't there to cover the event or interview the kids. It was just our small group doing something that may not have made the headlines, but did make a difference—at least to us and to the children and families we met that day.

As we started to say our goodbyes to each other, Mrs. Duff thanked me for having Hilary go with us and asked for my business card. When I referred to her as Mrs. Duff she replied, "Just call me Susan" and we continued to talk. She told me that Hilary had an older sister, Haylie, and the two girls were interested in acting. They were considering coming to Los Angeles and she wanted the girls to be involved in charity work. She shared with me some wonderful stories about previous holidays and their family tradition of doing for others.

She explained to me that when she invited friends to their house during the holiday season the question always came up, "What can I bring?" The response was not a traditional or expected one when Susan would say, "Just bring diapers, formula, bottles anything that we can give to a family in need." And that's just what they did. Haylie and Hilary recall their childhood holidays with fond memories. They remember seeing the smiles, hearing the laughter and sharing the happiness of the holiday season with families who had very little. Susan opened the doors of charity and her daughters experienced, at very young ages, important lessons that touched their hearts.

And Hilary's heart is truly full of compassion for others. She was then, the first day we met in Texas in 1997, and she is today, genuinely concerned about the well being of others. Over the years she oftentimes would ask me about specific children she had met and wanted to know how they were doing and if they were getting better. There were even times that she would become frustrated and wanted to know why, with all of our modern technology and research, we were unable to find a cure for specific diseases. She wanted everyone to have an opportunity to fulfill their dreams, whatever they may be, and live life to its fullest. She was a kid who cared and fortunately had a family who cared, too.

As I flew back to California I thought about Susan and Hilary and yes, I wondered if I would have a chance to work with them or even see them again. After all, I was from L.A. and familiar with people who talk the talk, as they say. I was hoping that this family would be different. I was hoping that they would call and really be interested in helping. Although I had a good feeling, I knew only time would tell. I would wait and see if they called once they arrived, settled in to their small apartment and started on that unpredictable road of the entertainment industry.

I also thought about the children and families we met and the laughter and smiles we shared. As I put my head back on the headrest of my coach class seat and closed my eyes, I could visualize many of the young patients' faces and remembered thinking, "I can't even imagine what they must be going through." I thought about healthy and active kids whose main concern was wondering what gifts would be waiting for them under their Christmas trees. I doubted whether there was even one small thought about the thousands of children who would be spending Christmas in a hospital bed. While the rest of the world was wrapped up with holiday festivities that would come and go, these young patients knew that every hour of every day counted.

I knew it was also an incredibly difficult time for the parents who had to face the reality that their child was battling a disease with no cure or an illness with no hope. The siblings, grandparents, aunts, uncles, cousins and friends were all spending the holiday season in a very different and painful way than most. Seeing and knowing this, I felt fortunate to be able to spend time with the children and families and share some very special and meaningful moments with them. And this was just the beginning of what I eventually came to realize was my life's passion and purpose.

I would continue to serve as the Executive Director of the Audrey Hepburn Children's Fund for the next year and a half. I certainly had no idea during this time that I would soon be creating my own non-profit children's charity, Kids With A Cause. I did not know what was in store for me nor could I have ever predicted the experiences that I would have or the thousands of children I would meet in the years to come. All I knew was that I wanted to continue to work with children. I wanted to do all that I could to teach kids to open their hearts to each other and make a difference in each other's lives. I wanted to build an organization that empowered youth and Kids With A Cause would be the next step that Hilary and I would take together.

Strange that we would meet in Texas, when my work was based in California, but not so strange when you think about how life unfolds to us each day. Out of thousands of people at "The North Pole Party", was it a coincidence that Hilary and Susan saw us and joined our group? Was it a coincidence that they had time and wanted to go with us to the hospital and visit the patients? Was it a coincidence that they were moving to Los Angeles? Was it a coincidence that we shared philanthropic interests?

You can call it what you want but I don't think it was a coincidence—I think it was a meant-to-be moment. And I cherish the first day that I was introduced to this beautiful little ten-year-old with a special sparkle. It was a day that I will always remember and an introduction to a little girl from Texas that touched my heart.

Chapter 2

Her Passion Brings Her To Hollywood

Hilary, happily participating in a food drive at a local store, takes time out to interact with a young child. The date was September 15, 2001 (the first weekend after the 9/11 tragedy) and Kids With A Cause not only collected food for the homeless in Los Angeles but also collected books and toys for the children in New York City.

Susan Duff, always ready to lend a helping hand, organizes program materials for Kids With A Cause. Our youth members and children from low-income families spent time together creating Thanksgiving baskets filled with food for the holiday.

♥

Lucky for Haylie and Hilary (and for all of us), it was decided that Susan would take the girls to Los Angeles to see if this "acting thing" (as Susan called it) was going to work out. She and her husband, Bob, discussed the potential opportunities for their daughters as well as the challenges and difficulties the family might face and tried to determine what would be best for all. Bob had a successful and growing business in Texas and, as a result, it seemed that the most logical decision was for him to continue to expand his business while Susan helped the girls pursue their acting careers.

Both Susan and Bob knew that this was something their daughters really wanted to try. After listening to the girls beg, bargain and plea for this hopeful acting break, the Duffs decided to let Haylie and Hilary experience this new and exciting adventure in Hollywood and see what happened. As loving parents, they felt it was important to give their children every opportunity to succeed in life, even if it meant moving to Los Angeles for a while and leaving family and friends back home in Texas.

The girls had an agent in Texas who supposedly had several auditions set up for them in Los Angeles, so they excitedly packed their bags, loaded the car and off to Hollywood they went. As it turned out, there really weren't *any* auditions set up for the Duff girls. Here they were in Los Angeles, new to the entertainment world and learning their first Hollywood lesson—that what is said may not always be true and often is misleading.

So, now what? Go back to Texas—oh, you don't know the Duffs! No, now is the time to take on the challenge and give it your all. Susan Duff bought book after book and began to learn all that she could about the business. Although she knew no one (especially in the entertainment industry), her warm and friendly easygoing personality started to open doors and she began to meet more and more people each day. She was getting her entertainment education through books and people and using her previous, and successful, business experience to make sense of it all. Eventually she met a Los Angeles agent who seemed just right for the girls. Haylie and Hilary then started just like everybody else with auditions, auditions, auditions.

Although the Texas agent was not a person true to his word, Susan Duff was, and still is. Soon after unpacking bags, hanging up clothes and moving a few personal items into their new apartment, Susan called my office to let me know that Haylie and Hilary were now in Los Angeles and ready to help out anytime. I was very pleased that she called and I explained the steps of program participation. Once I identified a recipient organization and developed the program, I would then contact the families of the young stars to determine who might be available for the date and time selected. I assured Susan that I would contact her when the next program or event was scheduled.

So while the Duffs were learning the ins and outs of Hollywood, I was researching and compiling the demographics of children in hospitals, group homes, homeless shelters and various other social service agencies to determine who and how the young stars of Hollywood could help.

Finding kids in hospitals, group homes or homeless shelters was easy—but oftentimes it was harder to schedule an event than I anticipated. You might be wondering "Who wouldn't want these up and coming young stars to come and interact with children, give them gifts, inspire and encourage them and offer them hope and happiness for a brighter tomorrow?" It was surprising how many phone calls, faxes and emails it would take sometimes before I would finally hear what I was waiting for, "Yes, we'd love to have your group visit our children." In most cases the hesitation was usually because they didn't know who we were or what we wanted to do. There were also concerns that many of the kids were very young (I was working with 6 to 18 year olds). These concerns, of course, all completely disappeared and turned into nothing but compliments once they met us and saw us in action.

I was determined to build the charity as an organization that could create opportunities for children to help children. I felt it was important to let them learn through personal experiences what lending a helping hand and making a difference really meant. I wanted kids like Haylie (who was 12½) and Hilary (who was 10) to meet and interact with kids who did not have the same opportunity or ability to fulfill their dreams because of various—and difficult—situations they faced.

As I began organizing numerous files of potential recipient organizations, I also started calling agents and mangers of young Hollywood talent. Not that I knew too many of the child stars or watched their shows, but I knew that somehow this special group of kids would make a difference to the children we would be meeting. Phone call after phone call, day after day, I finally started to figure out that since volunteer work is an unpaid job, it fell into the publicists' laps, rather than the agents or managers. Some publicists were very kind, some were not (another Hollywood lesson). When I explained what the charity was about and what I wanted to do, there were a few—I can count them on one hand—who said they would call their clients' families on my behalf and get back with me—and actually *did*.

One of the first programs I conducted was at a foster facility with children ranging in age from infants to twelve years old. It was the holiday season and plans for their annual foster family reunion were in place. They were pleased to have snacks, beverages, desserts and party decorations donated for the festivity. Since there wasn't enough money in the budget to cover everything, they did not have gifts to give the children.

I began to call companies and manufacturers to ask for new toy donations for this special occasion. Just as I discovered there were only a few publicists who were willing and interested in helping, I found much the same with the toy distributors. I did find, however, that if you ask enough people, someone somewhere is willing to help—especially if they know the items are for less fortunate children. I finally found a wonderful person at Mattel who was pleased to donate Hot Wheels for the boys and

Barbies for the girls. This was one of the first product donations I received and it was a very exciting day when the boxes arrived at my office and there were enough toys for all the foster children.

I was hoping to have at least two or three young stars from the entertainment industry that would be available and interested in participating. I began calling the publicists—starting with the cooperative ones. And I got lucky. One of the publicists called back to tell me that the girl she had in mind was planning to have a sleep over with a friend (who was also in the entertainment business) and wanted to know if they could both come to the foster family event. Well…yes! Two with one call; that's what I call double lucky.

The friend turned out to be Allison Mack, who is most recognized as *Chloe* on the hit series *Smallville*. From that day forward, Allison continued to work with me for several years until she booked her leading role on the series and moved to Canada to work. She was absolutely fantastic with the children and from the moment I met her it was obvious that she had a big heart and genuinely cared for children. Allison's smile would light up any room and soon she would have all the kids smiling, too. Allison Mack became the first Spokesperson for Kids With A Cause in the year 2000 and I was very proud to have her serve in this position as a strong, confident and positive role model for others. It was also exciting that many years later, Allison was able to take time and come to Hilary's Sweet Sixteen birthday celebration in Toronto and we were all reunited once again.

After this first program it became a little easier to call for young talent because now I could name drop about other young celebrities who were lending a helping hand. I was still calling the publicists and a few seemed *somewhat* interested. I think they were hoping that the media might be there and that it would be a good opportunity for their young clients. Others felt that whatever the families wanted to do on a volunteer basis was up to each individual family. As time went by, publicists stopped attending our charity events with their clients and this opened the door to direct communication with each young star and his or her family. And it certainly made my job a lot easier working directly with the kids and their parents.

Since the Duffs did not have a publicist at the time I met them in Texas and the initial contact was already made, I knew I could call Susan directly to schedule programs and events with Haylie and Hilary. And that's just what I did. Susan would listen to all the details, check the girls' schedules (because now they were beginning to book a few jobs) and confirm their participation. This was one family that I knew I could count on. They always showed up on time and were ready and eager to help, no matter where we went or what we did.

It took a dedicated effort along with a significant amount of time to schedule and organize program logistics, book the talent and develop programs for the recipient children. Although these interactive visits provided enriching and valuable philanthropic experiences, they did not generate revenue for the charity. Without a staff and only a few volunteers, it was difficult to coordinate and execute large fundraising galas. Although this may have been viewed as a challenge, there were still many other ways we were able to help and programs were implemented in California, Texas, New Jersey and New York. To increase awareness of the organization, as well as raise funds, we created an annual special event—the Academy Awards Benefit—designed for all ages. I discovered, however, at the next Board of Directors meeting that my journey in life would soon be changing.

The Board of Directors determined that my primary role would be fundraising. No more hospital visits, picnics with foster kids or holiday parties for kids and teens residing in group homes. My interactive work with kids was now secondary and the primary focus of my job was to create funding opportunities. After careful thought, I felt it best to resign from the position since it did not seem that it would fulfill what I truly wanted to do. I left on good terms and had no idea what I would do next.

There are some (very few) people I know that seem to always have the answer. And not just an answer, but the right answer for the right person. Somehow they are able to see the big picture and communicate a clear vision for others. Rod Jones, an international consultant, is one of those people. After sitting down with him and explaining that I was unsure what to do, but yet I knew what I loved, he simply said, "It's perfectly clear. You start your own charity." My immediate reaction was, "Oh, I can't do that" and then Rod talked me through each phase of concern I had. Every time I thought there was an obstacle in my path that would prevent me from this exciting opportunity, by talking out loud with him I found myself admitting that there really weren't any obstacles—except me. I had the experience, the knowledge and the compassion to take this new bold step. Nothing was stopping me, but me—and thirteen days later I incorporated the non-profit charity, Kids With A Cause, Inc.

Next was the challenge of telling the kids and the parents that I had been working with at the Audrey Hepburn Children's Fund about this new chapter in my life. I wanted them to continue their charitable efforts regardless of which organization they were willing to support. I sent a letter to all of them encouraging them to continue to help others. Without exception, all of the kids responded in a very favorable way and said that they wanted to continue to work with me and help kids in need. So Haylie and Hilary along with the others, decided to pursue hands-on charity work and experience the personal rewards of giving back.

I started Kids With A Cause with what I often refer to as my "S.O.S." (no Staff, Office or Salary). I was renting a home that had a guesthouse attached to the garage and I rearranged the guesthouse to become my first Kids With A Cause office. I worked with program volunteers, such as Susan Duff, and had a three-person Board of Directors. Even though we may not have had much in the beginning, we had what was most important – heart. We cared about everything we did and everyone we met.

Kids With A Cause was incorporated on September 13, 1999, and I knew that the holiday season was fast approaching, a time of year that was a busy one especially when working with children. With Thanksgiving just around the corner, I thought it would be good for the kids to understand that what many consider a traditional holiday feast was not always possible for homeless children and their families. I organized a program for the kids in our charity that would give them the opportunity to provide a Thanksgiving meal to those less fortunate.

The first step was to partner with a grocery store that would allow our charity to conduct a food drive and obtain the items we needed—and Whole Foods Market agreed. Kids With A Cause members volunteered their time and spent the day at the store describing our holiday project to the customers. The kids encouraged the shoppers to donate food for the Thanksgiving baskets we were going to create. The kids collected enough food to prepare fifty food baskets for families from homeless shelters who were now residing in temporary, low-income housing units.

From previous experiences with the kids, I found that personal interaction was an important factor in developing successful programs for them. Instead of simply putting non-perishable food items in baskets and delivering them to the families, I decided to turn it into a fun project that the kids, both the celebrity kids and those in temporary housing, could create together.

The Culver Studios graciously donated their back lawn area along with tables and tents to help us out. The recipient families were bussed to the studio and the children were each assigned a celebrity youth partner for the day. The teams were given an empty basket and a shopping list and were directed to the tables to "shop" (at no cost) until they found all the items on their lists.

After the baskets were stuffed with the traditional ingredients for a Thanksgiving meal, the children used colorful ribbons to wrap around the basket handles. They then spent time making cards for each other and writing special messages of thanks. As they exchanged their cards, it was clear that this day was meaningful to all and I knew, even from this first Kids With A Cause event, that having the opportunity to teach the principles and practices of philanthropy to today's youth was exactly what I wanted to do.

When they finished their Thanksgiving projects, the outdoor games began and it was a wonderful sight to see so many children running, playing and smiling. No matter who they were or where they lived, nothing seemed to matter except the fun they were having together.

As we said our goodbyes there were handshakes, hugs and high-fives. I was proud of the celebrity kids and how comfortable they were to meet a stranger and make a friend. We sat and discussed our day and how much it meant to give each family a Thanksgiving meal in a fun and meaningful way.

Susan loved watching her daughters take the hands of the recipient children and treat them with dignity, respect and admiration—despite the difficult times many of these children were facing. This, of course, was pre-*Lizzie McGuire* days and for Hilary it was a day that she could be just a regular kid. Her passion may have brought her to Hollywood, but her heart never changed after she arrived.

Chapter 3

It's All About Perception

The Duff sisters encourage and admire a young student feeding himself at a school for developmentally delayed children. Haylie and Hilary always helped brighten the day whenever they could for those less fortunate.

Haylie and Hilary, at the Kids With A Cause Academy Awards Benefit, show their excitement as they wait to meet the foster children they will be escorting on the red carpet entrance.

♥

So just how many times did Susan ask the girls, "Are you sure you don't want to go back and live a normal life in Texas?" More than once, that's for sure. Every time both Haylie and Hilary would look at Susan, look at each other and in unison reply, "Well,—*no-ooo*." So they decided to continue to pursue their acting careers, stay a bit longer and see what might happen. After all, they were now meeting more and more kids who were booking commercials, guest appearances and reoccurring roles. Who knew—maybe their turn would be next. If others could do it, why couldn't they? At least they could try.

They were now both going on several auditions but not booking every job, of course. They were beginning to realize, even at young ages, that the entertainment business is a competitive and tough industry filled with rejection. The love and support of a strong and determined mom helped them understand that this was all part of the business and that if a particular job didn't work out, something else would come along—in time. Susan helped them to remain positive, to look ahead and put the audition behind them. She helped them understand that if they didn't book a job it wasn't necessarily a reflection of their abilities. In fact, that may have had nothing to do with it at all.

Because of Susan's practical approach and advice, the girls never viewed rejection as a personal failure. They always tried their hardest and knew there were times the casting directors had a particular type or a specific look in mind for the role. But the girls never gave up. Who knew what might happen at the next audition? Who knew what job might be out there just waiting for them?

No one knows what the future holds and Hilary was certainly no exception. If she were asked at this time in her life what she thought she would be doing in the next five years she would never have imagined or said that she would be a world famous singer, actor, fashion designer, philanthropist—and more! She was a very happy teen trying her hand at acting and enjoying every minute of it.

After a lot more "nos" than "yeses" both the girls started to get callbacks and began to book a few jobs. Most of these beginning jobs were small parts on commercials or brief guest appearances on television shows but the acting bug was biting and they were thrilled when a job was offered to them.

Haylie and Hilary have always been extremely close sisters and even then, in the early stages of their acting careers, they were genuinely excited when one or the other would book a job. They were enthusiastic and supportive and always cheering each other on. As unusual as it may seem, they were not competitive with each other or jealous but instead each one was genuinely happy when good news arrived.

Yes, of course, there were times when Haylie or Hilary thought they had a great chance at a specific part. They felt their audition went well and it seemed that the production team thought they would be terrific for the role. The callback would then put them even closer to getting the part and their excitement would rise as they thought of the possibility that might be ahead.

Although they always did their best and "moved on" (as mom taught them), it wasn't always easy. Sometimes when they felt good and could visualize themselves playing a certain character, that part of the entertainment industry that every actor has to deal with, *"REJECTION"*, would boldly step in, center stage. It was especially difficult when the part was given to someone because of her height or hair or the fact that she had freckles. Yes, sometimes, it's really more about the look than the acting. But although they were both experiencing the rejection side of the business, they were still very happy to have the opportunity to try.

With each audition came more confidence and a better understanding of what Susan was trying to teach them. If they didn't get a callback Susan would tell the girls, "It's not a personal thing—there's probably something better out there for you." The girls believed that their mom was right and continued to view rejection as a part of life—especially an actor's life. After all, it's really the *perception* of rejection. And the Duff sisters remained upbeat and positive and continued to live their lives as "normal kids."

With true determination and lots of hard work they continued to walk through one audition door after the next. For Susan this wasn't an easy task either, since she had to drive both of the girls and juggle their schedules to ensure that they were where they were supposed to be at their designated call times. It wouldn't be too many more years before Haylie would be old enough to start driving and helping out. But for now the scheduling, the chauffeuring and the parenting were all up to Susan.

During this initial stage of their acting careers in Los Angeles, although they were keeping busy, they would always make time for our charity. They enthusiastically participated in every program and event they could and felt good about helping. They loved seeing the smiles and hearing the laughter from the kids we would visit. Susan was an excellent role model for the girls as she was always near by me ready to help with anything. She knew this hands-on experience of interacting with disadvantaged children and making a difference in their lives would have an important and lasting impact on the girls.

A key element of Kids With A Cause is not simply to invite our young members to participate in the fun of each program but also to give them an understanding of the work that is involved. I felt that by allowing them, and empowering them, to manage the programs from beginning to end would help instill strong leadership skills and important values. This educational approach could provide them with important "life lessons" such as team building skills, effective communication and personal accountability. They could learn about the business aspects of charitable work through these valuable behind-the-scenes experiences with their peers.

The Kids With A Cause members knew when they saw my car arrive at the designated facility that it was time to get busy. They would unload my car that was packed with everything we needed for the program, including art and craft supplies, gifts, clothing, books, CDs, educational materials and much more. I reminded the parents (who were always willing and eager to help) that it was *Kids* With A Cause, not *Adults* With A Cause and asked them to allow the kids to do this on their own, as it was part of the learning process.

By having the kids unload, carry and organize the items it also gave them an opportunity to see exactly what we would be giving to the kids. It was wonderful to see the excitement, knowing that soon these special toys and gifts would be in the hands of a child. Our youth members took great pride in making sure that everything was ready to go in a systematic way and organized the items according to gender and age. Every now and then I would hear a squeal of delight from one of them when "cool" toys were discovered. They were happy to be giving something that they knew the recipient kids were going to love. After all, they were kids too, and knew all about having fun.

Since the inception of Kids With A Cause, no two programs have been created exactly the same. We have conducted over 350 programs and events and interacted with thousands of children throughout the United States as well as six countries internationally. Prior to each event I would meet with the Kids With A Cause participants for a briefing session. These half-hour sessions were designed to discuss the program activities, describe our youth members' responsibilities and answer any questions they may have. This time also gave me an opportunity to provide an overview of the facility and its purpose and discuss the various reasons why the recipient children might require special care or need personal attention. These sessions helped our young members become aware of potential challenges they may face or sensitive situations that may arise.

An important part of the briefing session included the understanding that the recipient children might say things that, on the surface, could almost sound mean. It was essential to remind our kids about the *perception of rejection* and that unkind words should not be taken personally. I explained why these children were in their situations and how sad or painful it must be for those not living at home with their birth parents or those experiencing tough times. It was important to teach our kids to turn negatives into positives and to understand that the words spoken may not be the true intent of the message. I would give them examples of "words spoken but meanings meant" and demonstrate how to listen to what was said and then perceive it in a positive way. I let them know that it would take practice to perfect this skill and to always remember that negative messages were not meant to be personal criticisms.

And yes, there were times when one of the recipient kids would say something that could be taken wrong or perceived in a negative way. And each time our kids would smile and turn the negative comment into a positive one. It was great to observe this important interpersonal skill they were developing and to know that our kids were learning about the power of perception. The words spoken were not necessarily the words meant. They knew that the recipient children were going through difficult times and Kids With A Cause members always tried hard not only to listen to what was said but also to offer words of encouragement and support.

Each program would begin with an introduction of our charity, our kids and our purpose. To this day, the Kids With A Cause celebrity youth members always want me to introduce them because they don't like to talk about themselves or their accomplishments. They don't want to sound self-centered or to be viewed differently just because they work in the entertainment industry. Even during our programs, they never talk about themselves, their auditions or their work.

I knew, however, that it was important to the recipient kids to learn about these young actors and hear about some of their television and film appearances. There were numerous times I would hear the recipient kids say, "Oh, yeah, that's where I've seen you" or "I knew you looked familiar." Once the program and interaction began, there was never a separation or division of the two groups, but rather a room full of kids realizing they had a lot in common. They discovered there were more similarities they shared than there were differences.

Even though they found many common interests, it was all about perception. Many of the recipient kids felt they had done something wrong and it was somehow their fault that brought them to their undesirable situation. They perceived that, in some way, they caused the problem. Sometimes they wanted to talk about their personal situation and would tell us about the drug or alcohol problem of one or both of their parents or explain why their family was left homeless. Their perception of the situation was oftentimes self-blaming and resulted in a lack of confidence and low self-esteem.

On these occasions Kids With A Cause members would shine. I never prepared scripts for them to memorize or told them what to say, yet each and every time their messages were positive, powerful and encouraging. It seemed that they always knew just exactly what to say. It was free flowing communication from one kid to another. Their messages were genuine, heartfelt and definitely heard.

These special moments reinforced the entire reason that Kids With A Cause was created—to empower youth and motivate them to become people with passion. It was my hope that if even a small percentage of our celebrity youth members grew up with memories of these experiences, that perhaps these important philanthropic lessons would carry on into their adult years.

My desire was to continue to offer enriching experiences for children and teens and to encourage them to be caring and compassionate adults. I wanted to do all that I could to ensure that they had memorable experiences and multiple opportunities as young humanitarians. I felt that if the word spread and more people were inspired by our work, they might want to join us in our charitable efforts.

It was exciting to think that our small group of kids may actually have the ability to influence others and that someday children around the world may experience remarkable personal changes because of these young philanthropists.

Because of this desire as well as the perception of the organization, it was important to expand Kids With A Cause to include individuals outside of the entertainment industry. I started receiving emails, calls and letters inquiring about the charity and many included comments such as, "I'm not famous or on television but I still have a heart and want to help." It was at this time that I did not want Kids With A Cause to be perceived as a "celebrity only" charity. Just because the charity began with youth in the entertainment industry did not mean that it had to maintain an exclusive membership. I realized that there were kids everywhere that wanted to do their part and help, too.

By encouraging others to make a difference it also helped deliver the message that there are many ways to help. I emphasized to the kids that although all charities need money to operate, conduct programs and provide services, philanthropy comes from the heart and giving is personal. To many adults a philanthropist is most often described as a person who writes a donation check to a charity. To Kids With A Cause members, philanthropists are people who give their heart, their time, their care and concern to other individuals. The kids realized the importance and need for fundraising, but their focus was on personal interaction and time and time again they delivered messages of hope for a brighter tomorrow.

Once again, it is all about perception, even when it comes to philanthropy. What may be perceived as critically important to one person may not be viewed with the same importance to another. Some may consider fundraising as the measurment to non-profit success while others may feel that program achievements are what measure success. Kids With A Cause members recognized that inspiration, motivation and encouragement were important factors—without costs—that made significant differences and touched the hearts of children everywhere.

Although the art of giving is personal and different for each of us, the result is the same. When there is a smile on a child's face, or tears are wiped away and replaced with laughter, or arms are wrapped around you in a heartfelt hug—you know that you made a difference to this child at this time. After all, perception is how you choose to view a situation and the choice is yours.

Chapter 4

You've Got To Be Kidding – Me? Lizzie?

Hilary, as young *Lizzie*, attends an autograph signing to benefit Kids With A Cause and signs the handle of her unusual and fuzzy handbag.

Hilary, the loveable *Lizzie,* rides with Haylie in the Strawberry Festival Parade in Southern California. Her fans can't get enough of her, but this is only the beginning.

♥

So as time passed there were more auditions and more jobs for both Haylie and Hilary. With each job came more experience and more confidence. There were still, of course, several auditions that did not always result in work for the girls but they continued to look ahead in a positive manner for that next opportunity. And the Duff sisters knew by now that when opportunity knocked, they'd better be ready to open the door.

It was while Hilary was preparing for a toothpaste commercial she had booked that Susan received a call from their agent requesting that Hilary audition for a new Disney series. At that time the working title of the show was *What's Lizzie Thinking?* and her audition was for the lead role of *Lizzie*. The "sides" (the lines that must be memorized for the audition) were faxed to Hilary to learn prior to the audition. Since Hilary was busy working on the commercial she did not have as much time as she would have liked to learn her lines for the upcoming *Lizzie* audition.

The day of the audition came and Hilary put herself together in only a way that Hilary can. She coordinated her outfit and created a fun and playful—yet trendy—look. She mixed and matched layers, added lots of bangle bracelets and colorful hair accessories and then selected just the right shoes to pull everything together in her own unique way.

Although she showed up with a great look she didn't have her lines memorized as well as she could have, but as usual she decided to give it her best. While waiting for Hilary to finish the audition, Susan was checking her calendar and preparing for the days ahead to be sure that she could balance the girls' schedules. When the audition was over, Susan and Hilary got into the car and headed home. While driving, Susan asked Hilary how she did and Hilary responded, "I don't think I did too well. There were times that I forgot my lines and had to start over." Just as in the past Susan replied, "Well, don't worry. If this doesn't come through for you there's probably something better out there." And home they went.

The next day Susan's phone rang and it was a callback for Hilary for the role of *Lizzie*. It didn't mean that she got the part; it just meant that they wanted to see her again and have her read for the lead role. This was a step in the right direction and another opportunity for Hilary. Although Susan was somewhat surprised because of Hilary's comment about how the audition had gone, when she told Hilary about the callback Hilary was even more surprised and said, "You've got to be kidding—they want me back?!" This time Hilary really studied her lines and spent time *creating* the character that she was hoping would win her this leading role.

At the callback Hilary did a much better job and was much more prepared. Once again, she walked into the room with that special look that only she could capture. Hilary, having a strong interest in fashion, had an incredible ability to create her own look; a look that was sweet, clean and all American. She was the ideal role model that parents dreamed their children would look up to and emulate. She was clearly helping the producers, writers and animators define *Lizzie* with each step of the casting process.

It seemed that the callbacks went on and on. Hilary thought the reason was because this was a big Disney project and the casting directors and producers wanted to be sure that they found the right person for the part. Although what was really happening was that each callback was providing more insight to the production team about Hilary, her whimsical personality and her amazing concept of fashion. She was actually helping with the look of the animated *Lizzie* that was being created. Every outfit Hilary wore provided more ideas that helped develop the character.

It was while working on the toothpaste commercial that the day finally came and Susan's phone rang. She just heard the words that Hilary booked the lead role of *Lizzie* when Hilary entered the room. Susan said into the phone, "Would you mind repeating that?" and quickly handed the phone to Hilary. She heard the words for herself and with a look of amazement and a big, beaming smile—she let out a loud scream. Little did she know what was in store for her in the years to come and how this moment in time would be life changing for her.

As excited as she could possibly be, she couldn't wait to tell Haylie. This would be her first multi-year contract to play a leading character on a network with a worldwide audience. She loved the character and *Lizzie* and Hilary were sometimes inseparable. The show and the characters were further developed and the series was now simply titled *Lizzie McGuire*. As the scripts arrived each week, Haylie enthusiastically helped Hilary learn her lines. Hilary was excited to be working on a new and a fun television series, even though it was a lot of work and her free time was now very limited. Her personal time seemed almost non-existent as her work on the show, along with increasing publicity and media requests, was rapidly becoming more and more demanding and time consuming.

With the job of *Lizzie* came a lot of responsibility, especially for a young teen. When Hilary's friends would call and invite her to go to the mall or the beach or just hang out, there were many times that she was unable to join them because of her work. She never complained and felt very fortunate to have this exciting acting opportunity that had always been a dream of hers. She adjusted her life style and kept her commitment to always do her best. She showed up for work with a positive attitude and a willingness to devote long hours to ensure that each scene portrayed *Lizzie* in the way the director wanted.

As most people know, the *Lizzie McGuire* series turned out to be a runaway success. In fact it was so successful that it became Disney's Number 1 show, breaking many viewer ratings worldwide. And the television series was just the beginning. Soon to follow was the merchandise craze. *Everything* was *Lizzie*. The fans just couldn't get enough of her.

Books, stickers, dolls, games and what seemed to be an endless selection of *Lizzie* items did not sit on store shelves for long. *"Lizzie-mania"* was creeping across the globe and touching the lives of kids, preteens and teens everywhere.

Parents were also swept away by the clean image of Hilary. Her real life personality was much like her character. She was kind and sweet, fun and loving and, as with most "tweens", she had experiences of awkward, and even embarrassing not-sure-what-to-do moments. She (both on and off screen) had true compassion for others and always wanted to help if she could. In her own life Hilary was facing many of the same issues she was portraying as her character. This did not make her job any easier, it just helped her relate to certain situations because she understood them first-hand. She saw her character going through various stages of *growing up*, just as she was.

Hilary's viewpoint on fashion continued to be an integral part of the show. She loved the character's wardrobe and enjoyed adding her own touch, such as gluing fabric to headbands and adding rhinestones for an extra little flair. She was adventurous and yet conservative. She did not think it necessary (or even attractive) for teens to have to "show their skin" when putting a fashion ensemble together. She always seemed to have just the right look at just the right time—all the time.

Although she was as happy as she could be, her life was starting to change. She was now getting up very early, working every day and working hard. She studied her lines, attended school on the set every day, did her own stunts and happily fulfilled promotional requests and photo shoots whenever she was asked.

Even with her incredibly busy work schedule she still made time to help others and loved to do things to surprise me. One of the first big surprises came when she was only fourteen years old. Her mom had been contacted by a style publication that wanted to feature the *Lizzie* cast for their upcoming fashion catalog. Susan discussed the project with Hilary and explained how it would work, the amount of pay for the job, the hours and other details so that Hilary knew what was ahead for her. As she listened to her mom discuss the opportunity, she was excited and thought it sounded like it would be fun. When the topic of pay came up Hilary did not hesitate and simply said to her mom, "That's cool, but I don't really want the money for me. Why don't we give it to Linda?" And that's what they decided to do—without telling me. They asked the project director about their request and were told that it would not be a problem. Susan and Hilary asked that the check be made payable to Kids With A Cause, Inc. and delivered to my office prior to the shoot date.

As the weeks passed, Kids With A Cause did not receive the promised check. The day before the scheduled shoot the creative director was going over the elements of the photo session with Susan. She looked up and simply said, "Well, my daughter won't be there." Seeing looks of shock and disbelief she continued with, "We only asked for one thing. We asked that Hilary's pay was written to Kids With A Cause and delivered before we began shooting." At this point it suddenly became clear that this one request from the Duffs had not been fulfilled.

Susan is a woman of her word and expects that others be, too. She had not asked for something that was impossible or even difficult to do. Yet somehow this issue was not addressed and now time was running out since the photo shoot was scheduled for the next day—only now without *Lizzie*—rather, Hilary. Since the fashion catalog needed the show's main star, everyone now began to scramble. The situation was something that needed to be resolved, even at the eleventh hour, and requests to fulfill this passed from one person to another. Luckily there was an executive on the Disney set who stepped in to help out. The check was written and delivered by messenger to my office late that afternoon.

When I received the delivery I wasn't sure what it was and upon opening the envelope and seeing what was inside, I felt my heart begin to pound much faster. I didn't recognize the individual or the company the check was from but based on the amount, I knew that Hilary was somehow involved.

I immediately called the set and Susan answered the phone. I frantically said, "Something very strange just happened. I received an envelope with a check. A sizeable check. At first I thought it was delivered to the wrong company but it's made out to Kids With A Cause. We've never received an unexpected check like this and I don't want to get too excited because I'm afraid there might be a mistake and that it's not intend for our charity." She gave a sweet little laugh and just then Hilary walked into her production trailer and Susan said, “Hil, pick up the phone.” We greeted each other on the phone and I proceeded to tell Hilary that I thought I might need to call 9-1-1 because I just received this very generous “surprise” and my heart was racing. Hilary just laughed and said, “Oh, did you get the check?” Within a few minutes she was called back on set and said, “I have to go now—I love you.” and off she went. Susan then told me the whole story and explained that it was Hilary’s idea to donate the money. Although I was surprised, I wasn’t. That’s just how the Duff family is.

Another surprise for the charity was the donation of the leopard print jacket that Hilary wore on the final callback when she found out she booked the job. It was her lucky jacket and she was willing to donate it to Kids With A Cause as an auction item to raise money and help kids. When she decided to donate this special jacket, I wanted to be sure that it wasn’t something that she might regret giving up someday. I said, “You know, Hilary, this is a very special jacket for you. There’s only one and what if someday you want to give it to your children or keep it for yourself. I don’t want to take something that you may decide later on in life is important to you.” She simply replied with “Linda, it’s just a thing; a piece of clothing. I would rather give it to you and raise money to help kids.”

And, of course, her giving didn’t stop there. Whenever Hilary cleaned out her closet she’d pack big plastic bags full of her personal clothing and I would drive to her house to pick them up. She liked to pick out special things for me, too, that she thought would be cool and put them in a separate bag. Yes, I am lucky that some of her jackets, shirts and shoes are just my size.

One time she gave me a beautiful black suede jacket with silver stud accents. She had worn it on the show in one of the episodes and loved it. She never dreamed that she would actually get to keep it so she bought an identical one for herself. When the show wrapped, the black suede jacket was given to her. She decided to give the one she had purchased to me. So we both had the same jacket—and I still have mine to this day.

I always enjoyed going over to the house and spending time with the Duffs. Susan is a great cook and could whip up a delicious dinner while juggling at least three or four other things at the same time. Whenever I would ask if she needed help in the kitchen, she never did. She had it all under control and simply asked that I join her so that we could talk while she finished the last minute preparation. She would ask the girls to help set the table and get the serving dishes. Susan made me feel right at home and we all enjoyed our time together.

Haylie and Hilary also took care of feeding the dogs, cleaning their rooms and other normal teenage chores. They were being raised to be responsible individuals and were not given special treatment because they were now doing this "acting thing." It was important to Susan that the girls were well mannered and polite, independent, responsible and caring people. She never asked for anything special for Hilary or Haylie when they were working. There were no special requests that must be fulfilled.

Susan felt that the girls should always do the best they could at whatever project or job they were working on at the time. She did not ever ask for "star" treatment for them.

The *Lizzie* contract was for four years, sixty-five episodes. Even with the success of the show, the producers knew that the main characters would soon be growing up and would no longer be able to play the young ages they were initially cast for in the series. There was talk of renewing the series with *Lizzie* going on to high school, which would allow the same cast to continue and portray the older ages of high school students. This was a critical point in Hilary's life because she had to think about committing to the series for another four years in the *Lizzie* role or moving on to explore other opportunities.

The big question was *what should she do*? What would be next? What if there wasn't another successful series for her? What if she was now typecast as *Lizzie* and not known as Hilary? What if her fans were disappointed in her decision? What if breaking away from the young *Lizzie* role and emerging on the independent talents of Hilary were not accepted? What would be next for Hilary Duff, the young talented star of *Lizzie McGuire*? Only time would tell and what a story it would be.

Chapter 5

Dreams Really Can Come True

This young fan admitted that he had a "crush" on Hilary. When he met her, she gave him a sweet little kiss on the cheek. He wrote me a letter and said, "It was the greatest night of my life."

Hilary (looking as gorgeous as ever) wearing her *Cinderella* ballgown and making dreams come true for Kids With A Cause guests at a special screening of the film.

As more and more talks went on about the possibility of a continued older version of the *Lizzie* series, Hilary had time to think about what she wanted to do. She loved the show and her character and really enjoyed all the great times she had while working on the series. She was concerned though that another four years was a long time and that she would not be able to pursue any of her other dreams. It was a big decision to make.

Her mom helped her by talking about various aspects that might be ahead yet also letting her know there would be risks ahead, too. The *Lizzie McGuire* series gave her worldwide fame but would she be able to stand on her own apart from *Lizzie*? Would it be a good decision to decline the offer at this point in her career?

Her fans, of course, wanted her to continue with the popular Disney show. They wanted to share the high school drama that *Lizzie* would experience. This, too, was difficult for Hilary because in many ways she felt the same as her fans. It would be great to continue and experience the adventures of *Lizzie* in high school. On the other hand, it would also be exciting to experience some other interests of hers including acting in feature films, designing clothes, continuing with her education and so much more.

Susan attended several meetings with the producers to listen to the discussions of the proposed extended series. She was open to hearing what was planned. She and Hilary wanted to be certain that the commitment as well as the options were clear to them. Although many people disagreed with the decision, the Duffs felt it was best, for many reasons, to move on—and so they did.

The big step from *Lizzie* had now been taken and it was important that Hilary establish herself as *Hilary*. There were many projects and plans in the works but the question still remained—would the public know Hilary Duff or *Lizzie McGuire*? It wouldn't take long for the millions of fans who adored her to learn that *Lizzie* was Hilary Duff and her individual fame began to blossom as a multi-talented young person.

Her acting on the big screen expanded her experience from television and Hilary loved it. From *The Lizzie McGuire Movie* to *Agent Cody Banks*, Hilary's dream (at least one of them) was beginning to come true. Her decision to work as an independent actor was allowing her enormous fan base to continue to see her, love her and learn more about her as *Hilary* rather than *Lizzie*. She was beginning to be recognized for who she was not just as an extension of the character she had been playing.

With several television and film projects in 2003 alone, Hilary Duff was in high demand. Script opportunities were coming to her on a regular basis and she was in a position that allowed her to select projects that were of interest to her. The decision to move on was the right one. There was no turning back for Hilary and doors were beginning to open that inspired her to do even more.

One day while driving in the car with her mom, Susan said, "Hey, Hil, how would you like to be a pop star?" Hilary looked at her with her big hazel eyes and said, "Well, mom, I think it'd be cool but I haven't taken voice lessons and I'm not sure - - " Before she even finished her thought her mom replied, "Well, if you want to, we can find a voice coach for you." Hilary, as always, was eager to explore new opportunities and this facet of entertainment was especially interesting to her. She thought that singing would be fun although she had no idea what this decision would mean or what was ahead for her.

Susan Duff, with a tremendous ability to find the right person for the right job, did exactly that for Hilary. From vocal coaches to music managers, songwriters to producers, it was all starting to come together without too many people knowing about it. I remember going over to their house one night and Susan and I were going to go out to dinner. When we got in her car she put on a demo CD that Hilary had recorded. This was the first time I heard Hilary sing and she sounded fabulous. She had her own upbeat, individual sound and sang her meaningful lyrics with passion. Susan and I were both smiling because it meant that a new adventure might be ahead.

When we returned to the house that night Hilary was back from her music rehearsal. Susan told her that we listened to the demo CD and Hilary seemed a bit apprehensive about what my reaction might be and softly said, "Oh, you did." I told her I thought she sounded great and how excited I was for her. I enthusiastically let her know that I would be one of the first people to buy her CD when it was released. She gave me that beautiful smile followed by a little giggle and said, “Oh, thanks. I still have a lot of work to do, but it’s fun.”

Susan had purchased a small electric keyboard for Hilary that was in the corner of the living room. She asked Hilary to play and sing for me. It was one of those moments that I’ll never forget. Hilary stood behind the keyboard all by herself and sweetly sang *Come Clean.* She only sang part of the song but enough for me to know that she was headed in a new and exciting direction. At that time she was unsure of herself as a music artist but she was having fun and loved singing. How I wish I had videotaped that special night watching and listening to Hilary, a young teen, about to embark on the music scene.

More hard work, and lots of it, was ahead for Hilary. She had voice lessons, songwriting sessions, meetings with music producers and practice, practice, practice. She was not sure that her television and film fans would accept her as a singer and she wanted to be sure that her songs were not only right for her voice but also delivered positive and influential messages. She wanted her music to mean something. It was critically important to her that she was involved with the selection of songs and lyrics as well as the pop star image she would portray. She wanted to connect with her audience and be someone they could relate to. Music was a new world and a bold step for Hilary and she was the first to admit that she was nervous about her fans’ reaction to this new venture. She worked incredibly hard to become the multi-platinum recording artist that she is today.

Andre Recke, a successful and talented music executive, became her music manager. He scheduled her first live performance in Hawaii just before her 16th birthday. Hilary had her friends and family with her for support. The outdoor venue that was selected was intentionally small to let Hilary experience a live audience and sing on stage for the first time. Still unsure of the reaction to her as a singer, Hilary was very nervous about her first live performance. At one point she actually thought she was going to be sick but realized it was just nerves and, as always, she was determined to go on stage and perform her best.

When her fans heard her sing they went wild. They loved her. She could not have made them happier and for Hilary it was a real boost to her confidence to be accepted, at least for this initial show, as a singer. Now the question was, would she be able to continue to gain credibility as a music artist and perform to sell-out crowds (and we all know the answer to that).

Hilary's fans knew this was a new experience for her and they were enthusiastic and eager to hear her. There was something very special about her songs and her sound that set her apart from others who were at the top of the record charts. But even with a great response and tremendous interest from her fans, Hilary and Susan both felt that it wasn't time yet for Hilary to perform to large audiences. Hilary wanted to spend the time she needed to select the right songs and record her first CD. She wanted to spend more time in the studio with more coaching and practice, more rehearsals with her band and more time to get herself ready for this big career step.

Although Andre was guiding her and helping her establish herself as a music performer, Hilary had input in both the songs and the lyrics. It was important that she liked what she was singing and that the words meant something to those listening. It was decided that she would record and release a single from her first CD and see how she did. *So Yesterday* not only hit Number 1 but also became a household phrase. Everyone was now watching and listening to Hilary Duff—the pop star!

After the release and success of her first CD, *Metamorphosis*, it was evident that singing was not only exciting for Hilary but also for millions of her fans worldwide. People were listening to her CD over and over again and watching her music videos every chance they could. Hilary Duff was rocking the world. Everyone was waiting for her first concert tour, which was soon to come.

For a teenager, especially one that was not known (yet) for her singing, performing in front of a packed venue with thousands of people could be a terrifying thought. Yet for Hilary, she was motivated and determined to work even harder and prove that she could take on this new challenge. Every element was important to her including the people who would be in her band. As unusual as it might sound, she was looking for honest, clean image, drug-free musicians (yes, there are actually some) and people she knew she could count on to help her achieve this new level of success. As the band members came together, so did the music. The look and sound that was being created would soon become world famous.

Andre was preparing Hilary and her band for a successful tour and was beginning to look for appropriate concert venues. He and Susan felt that initially it would be better to have smaller performance centers that were packed rather than larger ones with empty seats. At this time they, too, were unsure how Hilary's fans would react to her as a music performer.

After months and months of rehearsals, negotiating logistics and contracts, designing the stage and special effects elements, creating concert merchandise, promoting and publicizing the tour and ZILLIONS of other details—Hilary was ready for the road. Her first tour was about to begin and it was time for her fans to fasten their seat belts.

I can't tell you exactly how many of Hilary's concerts I attended over the years, escorting special guests, but I would estimate somewhere between thirty to forty. At every concert the fans screamed with delight when they saw and heard Hilary. It was easy to see that they were having the time of their lives, enjoying every single minute and wishing the evening would never end.

Susan and I oftentimes stood under the ramps of Hilary's stage and watched her perform. It was amazing to look out into the audience and see thousands and thousands of people (from the seats at the highest level to those in the front row) waving their Hilary Duff light sticks and hearing them sing the words to her songs. It was a remarkable experience and one that certainly proved that Hilary's fans not only accepted her as a singer; they *loved* her music.

With each passing year Hilary became more and more confident and her comfort level, as well as her enjoyment, was obvious. She had, once again, found that hard work and determination were critical to her success. Her schedule was now becoming a challenging balancing act between singing and acting.

And even though she loved doing both, she also loved fashion—so why not create her own clothing designs? And that's just what she did. *Stuff by Hilary Duff* was the name of her new clothing brand that she created for young girls and preteens. It took a tremendous amount of work and dedication but if you knew Hilary, you would know that the thought of hard work doesn't stop her.

She wanted to have input, just as with her other projects, on her clothing line and ensure that each item had her personal touch. She wanted to select the right fabrics, the right colors and of course, create the right styles. She was involved with every detail including the fashion show launch of her newly created styles. It took a long time from the original sketches to the final production but it was a proud moment for Hilary to watch the young models wearing the clothes she had designed.

Hilary also made sure that everything was not just fashionable but affordable, too. It was important to her that the stores carrying her clothing were not high-end department stores but rather stores that carried products for families on moderate budgets. Many stores would sell their entire *Stuff by Hilary Duff* inventory soon after the arrival of a new shipment, due to the high demand of her brand.

Although her new clothing line was wildly popular, Hilary's belief was that fashion and accessories go hand in hand. She also felt that every girl could have fun with cosmetics, even if it was simply a little lip-gloss for the young ones or nail polish for the preteens. Hilary was having a great time creating these fun fashion accessories and it seemed that everything she wanted to do was working out for her and her success continued to escalate. She felt fortunate to experience these great opportunities in her life and share her interests with her fans. As she would always say, "I'm just a regular kid but I'm so lucky that I get to do all these things."

I always believed it was more than just luck. I have never known an individual (including many adults) who find their passion at a young age and are willing to pay the price of hard work to see their dreams turn into reality. Hilary never complained about the long days, the non-stop schedule, the little (if any) time she had to spend with her friends. She did what had to be done everyday. And she did it with a positive attitude. She knew that it would take hard work if she was going to fulfill her dreams and she was willing to put in the time and the effort.

During this seamless transition from *Lizzie* to Hilary, even with an incredibly busy schedule,

Hilary always thought of Kids With A Cause and found ways she could continue to help. Our charity was fortunate to receive hundreds of items of her clothing, footwear, cosmetics and accessories that we could give to children in need. As her dreams were coming true, she was also helping to make the dreams of others come true, too. There were always smiles and giggles when a little girl became the proud owner of one of Hilary's special gifts.

Hilary also took time to personally sign items for Kids With A Cause to auction and raise funds for less fortunate youth and teens. Over the years she has given our charity signed scripts, handbags, jackets, CDs, DVDs, posters and many other valuable items. Even though (with her popularity increasing) she wasn't able to attend our events as often as she could in the past, she continued to support our efforts with these personally signed items.

Hilary was inspiring millions of kids and teens around the world and became a positive role model for them. She was not just viewed as an actress, singer and fashion designer but also as a person with a kind and caring heart. Kids With A Cause began to receive more phone calls, emails and letters everyday about the wonderful charitable attributes of Hilary and it was becoming obvious, at least to me, that she was influencing today's youth and positively impacting them. She was encouraging others to do their best, believe in themselves, never give up and follow their dreams. She was also delivering the message that "everybody can do something to help someone else." This was truly a young lady whose heart of gold was seen by all.

Every day was a busy day for Hilary and she couldn't have been happier. She loved working, especially since no two days were ever alike. When she would wake up in the morning she would ask, "So what's happening today?" No matter what the answer was, she was always up for the challenge and was a very happy teenager proving that dreams really can come true.

Chapter 6

Keep Believing And Keep Achieving

Hilary has a great sense of humor and believes in having fun. Here she is with a special guest "hamming it up" for the camera.

Hilary loves to make kids smile and after a serious photo, she would often tell them to make a "silly face." In this case, it was only Hilary that decided to go along with the gag.

♥

Were there skeptics out there? Were there critics who wrote unfavorable reviews about Hilary's singing? Were there people who thought maybe she got lucky on the success of her first CD and that would be it? Of course there were. Did any of this uncertainty or doubt change Hilary's mind about her music—of course it didn't. Hilary's fame as a music artist was sweeping across the globe with the loyal support of her fans.

As her tour dates were announced and tickets went on sale, there were many times that Hilary's concerts would sell out in sometimes just a matter of minutes! She was definitely one of the "Most Wanted" artists and was appealing to a wide population from young kids to grandparents. Many of her fans had never been to a concert before and they were there to enjoy the sights and sounds of Hilary with their parents. It was amazing to watch the enormous crowds, to look out at the massive number of posters, banners and signs, to watch the parade of *Stuff by Hilary Duff* outfits and to see the beautiful bouquets of flowers and special gifts her fans brought her. But the best part of it all was seeing happy and excited children whose lives and hearts she touched in a very meaningful way.

Kids With A Cause was fortunate to have the Duff's continued support especially when it came to obtaining Hilary Duff "Most Wanted" concert tickets. It was a privilege for our charity to become the liaison between the Duffs and various wish granting organizations. We were able to help fulfill the dreams and wishes of terminally ill children who wanted nothing more than to meet their idol and see her perform. Fulfilling these wishes became a time consuming, yet very rewarding, part of my job.

Each ticket request had to be submitted in writing to our office from the established wish granting organization along with accompanying medical documentation. This process helped ensure not only that the request had not been previously fulfilled for the same child, but also helped to identify any medical or physical challenges that may require accessible seating. Susan and I would go over the list of requests and she would allocate the necessary tickets for each city on the tour. She also wanted me to make sure that the Kids With A Cause guests were escorted to the front of the Meet & Greet line since many of them were in wheelchairs or were too frail to stand in line waiting for long periods of time.

The Meet & Greet was always prior to the concert and many of the kids waited for this special moment with almost uncontrollable excitement. They couldn't believe that soon they were actually going to meet their favorite star. While waiting, I would talk to our group of guests about Hilary and answer some of the behind-the-scenes questions they were curious about including "Are her dogs with her?" or "What will she be wearing?" or "What songs will she be singing?" It seemed that no matter what trivia question I would ask them about Hilary, such as where she was born or the names of her parents, every fan knew the answers. Hilary was an important part of their lives and they were watching, reading and listening to all the news and finding facts and information about their idol—this world famous star.

As the minutes would go by the anticipation and excitement would grow until finally her tour team would come into the Meet & Greet room to tell us she was on her way. There were actually a few occasions that some of her fans would be so overwhelmed at the thought of meeting her that they would get butterflies in their stomachs and throw up. But that didn't stop them from standing firm in line until it was their turn to share this magical and unforgettable moment with her.

At every concert, without fail, Hilary would walk into the Meet & Greet room with her radiant smile and upbeat personality. She showed genuine interest in meeting our new friends and spending time with them. She would look them in the eye and talk to them before the keepsake Polaroid picture was snapped. Many of her fans brought her gifts and cards and she was always very touched. Often times she would put on a bracelet or necklace her fans gave her at the Meet & Greet and wear it during her concert performance. What an incredible experience it was for these special kids to see how much their thoughtful gifts meant to Hilary and watch her wear something on stage that night that they had just given to her.

Every guest was important to Hilary. She would take time to interact with them, ask them questions and facilitate one-on-one conversations. During those moments it was almost as if there was no one else in the room. They then posed for a photo together and Hilary would give our special guest a big hug. She was always sure to thank each person for coming to her show.

Whenever possible, she would offer words of strength and encouragement and remind these special fans to keep believing in their dreams. She made sure to tell them that she would look for them during the show. And she did. There were many times that once she saw them she would walk to the edge of the stage to reach down and touch their hands or wink at them or blow them a kiss. This was a magical moment and many of our guests screamed when this happened and told me they would never wash their hands again because of her special touch. She made every child feel important and close to her.

There were also times when I would sit with Hilary in her dressing room after the Meet & Greet and we'd talk. She was always very concerned about the health and well being of the kids and would ask me questions about their medical conditions. She often would ask, "With all the medical technology and research, why can't they find a cure?" She knew how fortunate she was and she did not like to see others suffer. Although she was meeting new kids each week, she held a special spot in her heart for each of them and made every effort to let them know she cared.

She also was imparting key messages to her audiences about helping others. She was strong in her belief that everyone can make a difference and emphasized that together we can achieve important goals and help to make the world a better place. No matter where she traveled she took time to explain that it didn't take a lot from one person to make a difference, but that a little from a lot of people could.

Hilary was discovering the power she had to create change and was encouraging her fans to do their part and help, too. She was one person, even though she was a teenager, that millions of people listened to and looked up to with admiration and respect. She had devoted fans that were willing to do what they could and lend a helping hand in any way possible.

At one concert there was a young girl in the audience who was holding up an over-sized check written to Kids With A Cause. This elementary grade school student (along with some help from her mom) created a fundraising campaign "Get, Give and Ask" and formed a group that worked together on this special project. The goal for each student was to earn $5.00 ("Get"), donate $5.00 ("Give") and then approach someone else to match the $5.00 donation ("Ask"). Through this unique fundraising program these young students were able to expand their charitable efforts to others and collected $250 to donate to our charity. This was another great example of believing and achieving —by grade school students.

Susan Duff, who was standing behind the stage, happened to see this young girl holding up the check. After the concert Susan asked a member of the tour team to see if this child and her mother would like to come back stage and meet Hilary.

Susan told Hilary about the check and Hil was very touched. She wanted to thank this young fan personally and she did. This, of course, was certainly a big surprise, very unexpected and very welcomed by the girl and her mother. Pictures were taken followed by hugs and words of appreciation. Hilary expressed her gratitude and commented on the wonderful and kind gesture as she accepted the check on behalf of Kids With A Cause. She also shared her philosophy that if you keep believing, you can keep achieving. This young girl continued her philanthropy work and she and her mom eventually established a non-profit charity modeled after Kids With A Cause.

Hilary's charitable work with Kids With A Cause was beginning to spread to all parts of the world. More and more emails, cards, letters and phone calls were coming to our office from kids and parents wanting to know what they could do or how they could help. They were watching Hilary and hearing her philanthropic message as she encouraged everyone to get involved. One first grade student sent in an adorable drawing of Hilary. In the envelope there were also pennies, nickels and dimes that totaled thirty-seven cents. Included was a short note: "I saved my money to help kids and I want Kids With A Cause to have this."

A caring teenager made and sold holiday crafts and donated the money to Kids With A Cause to help purchase gifts for children in hospitals. Another sweet and thoughtful child sent one toothbrush with a note stating, "I know it's not much, but at least it's a start. I'll try to send more stuff soon." It was obvious to me that Hilary's heart was coming through to people loud and clear. Her fans recognized her acts of kindness and generosity and they wanted to be like her and make a difference, too.

When the media interviewed Hilary it was usually *not* about her charitable work. Most of the press were more interested in her personal life, her love interests or her next film, but rarely was there talk of her compassion and desire to lend a helping hand to children in need. On the rare occasions that the topic of charity would come up, Hilary spoke of her first-hand experiences with Kids With A Cause and what it meant to her to be able to put a smile on a child's face. She took these media opportunities to continue to encourage others to do what they could to bring hope and happiness to those less fortunate.

Hilary was a charter member of Kids With A Cause and a strong believer in our charitable work. She truly enjoyed having the opportunity to interact with recipient kids. Although her schedule was extremely busy she did what she could, when she could, to brighten the lives of others. Even while touring she tried to make time (whenever possible) to visit children who were hospitalized and couldn't go to her concert. These personal in-room visits were brief but had exciting and lasting memories for the pediatric patients.

On one occasion there was a young teen, who was a big fan of Hilary's, that was diagnosed with kidney failure and her future did not look good. Before the concert that night I made arrangements for Hil to meet me at the hospital and spend a few minutes with this young patient. Hilary and I went through the back entrance of the hospital, where she wouldn't be seen, since there was not enough time for her to visit or even say hello to each patient and she didn't want to hurt anyone's feelings.

The young patient was not told of Hilary's visit and when we entered the room it was a big surprise. The young girl could barely believe that Hilary was right there in her room! Hilary autographed some keepsake items and sat on the hospital bed talking with the young patient. Hilary gave her a concert program and told her she would be thinking of her that night. The patient's father, who knew about the surprise visit, took pictures of the girls together. Hilary encouraged the young girl to stay strong and be brave—and off she went to perform.

Several weeks later I received a letter from the girl's father. His daughter had received a new kidney—just in time—and was on the road to recovery. He said in the letter that he had never seen his daughter so happy as the night she met Hilary. Her attitude was positive and she was somehow able to hang on until a perfect match was found for the organ transplant that she desperately needed. He credits much of his daughter's strength to Hilary and was very touched by the kindness she extended to their family.

Hilary was touching the hearts of everyone. Her fan base was expanding and included people as young as the *Lizzie* followers to college students and beyond. She was setting an amazing example of what could be accomplished by believing in something and taking steps to achieve it. Her message to do something, even in a small way, was raising awareness and influencing others to take action.

Because of Hilary's positive impact, a college student decided to do something special for Valentine's Day on her school campus. She made heart-shaped pins with the words "I am loved" in nine different languages to sell for one dollar and support Kids With A Cause. Her fundraising campaign was so successful that nearly all the students in the small college donated their dollar and wore their pins that day. This sophomore student was written up in the local newspaper along with a photo of her and the fundraising pins she designed. Her thoughtful and heartfelt efforts raised over $700 for our charity.

Although Hilary had a tremendous impact on others there were also people that she looked up to who inspired her by their actions of great bravery, courage or determination. One of the world's greatest individuals with these unwavering qualities, Nelson Mandela, was one of them. He believed and achieved more than what seemed to be humanly possible and Hilary and I would soon have the rare opportunity to meet him.

It all started with a phone call I rceeived from an event planner in New York City. He began to tell me about a program called "Say Yes For Children." The program had a basic premise: ten fundamental rights for all children worldwide. The objective was to encourage people to vote "yes" to these crucial rights, by using computer technology, and obtain millions of votes from children and adults around the world.

Kids With A Cause eagerly agreed to promote the campaign on our website and do what we could to encourage people to vote and "Say Yes For Children." A few days after the initial call I received another call from the event organizers regarding their plan to announce the total number of votes to prominent leaders of the world. This announcement, presented to the Heads of State, diplomats and dignitaries, was going to take place at the United Nations Building in New York City—and this call was to invite Hilary to host this prestigious program and be an important part of this history-making moment.

In addition to the announcement of the voting results, the program would also include several very talented and highly entertaining youth performers from all parts of the world. Dressed in their traditional and colorful clothing, they were prepared to provide song and dance for this notable gathering of world leaders. This special session, presented by kids on behalf of kids, was the first function held at the UN since the terrible tragedy of 9/11.

It was while we were conducting the dress rehearsal that I saw Nelson Mandela and Kofi Anon escorted into a private area. I felt that since Hilary was hosting the event and introducing each program element to this prestigious audience, it would be important for her to meet these two highly respected men to whom she would be speaking to that evening.

This introduction was not an easy task, however, because of the high level of security. Being the determined person I am, I believe anything is possible and *where there's a will, there's a way.* Within a few minutes I approached one of the secret service individuals to find out how to fulfill my request. He told me to check with another individual and this task of going from one person to the next continued until I finally found the right person. As I was directed to "the lady in the red jacket" I introduced myself to her and told her of my desire to allow this special meeting for Hilary. The woman was very polite and agreed to allow us into the private area for a brief moment.

Susan was on her cell phone on a business call when I turned and looked at her and said, "I'm taking Hilary in to meet Nelson Mandela and Kofi Anon." Susan's eyes were as big as could be and she couldn't believe that Hilary was going to actually have the opportunity to meet men of such stature. She smiled because she knew this would be a very memorable moment for her daughter.

Before we stepped inside I explained to Hilary that we would only have a few minutes to meet them. I suggested that she observe and reciprocate with whatever gesture was extended to her whether it was a handshake or simply a verbal greeting. As the secret service personnel opened the door and we entered the area, I was very surprised to find only three people inside: Nelson Mandela, Kofi Anon and Mrs. Anon. I introduced Hilary to them and explained her role in the special session meeting. They all smiled and stood up to thank her for hosting the program and for her support on behalf of the children of the world. These three distinguished individuals extended their hands to Hilary, she followed their lead, and politely shook hands with them. We spent only a few minutes in this very private area but it was a few minutes that will never be forgotten by her or by me.

Due to last minute program changes, the event producers had to revise Hilary's script multiple times that night even with just seconds before she was supposed to go on stage. I stopped counting after nine script changes and knew that she was a professional and would be able to make the necessary adjustments. It was no surprise to me that she performed beautifully and the program was flawless. She was a fun and gracious host and enthusiastically introduced all of the outstanding youth entertainment perfectly, even though many of their names were extremely difficult to pronounce. Her mom and I sat together and watched this historic event unfold. The people of the world responded and it was revealed that more votes were cast in favor of "Say Yes For Children" than any other online campaign ever before.

Once again, Hilary proved that if you believe you can achieve. She was faced with an exciting, yet challenging, opportunity to host this special session. She knew she had only one chance to do her best because, unlike television, this was live and there would not be an option to re-do scenes. She had to believe she could achieve—and she did.

Hilary Duff

Over the years, Hilary signed several photos including this one at age 11. Her message meant a lot to me and also said a lot about her. At this time she used a heart symbol along with the words "love you."

Hilary's growing up and her signature is becoming more sophisticated. She wasn't sure if she spelled "role model" right and apologized for writing over the letters to correct them. This was one of the few autographs that she used "XOXO" (which her mom uses on emails) instead of her heart symbol.

At age 13, Hilary's a rising star and writes, "Kids (Kids With A Cause) Rocks" along with her heartfelt message. She's a warm and caring person with a big heart and once again, uses her heart symbol above her signature.

Cadet Kelly
L to R: Hilary Duff, Christy Carlson Romano

Hilary, at age 14, adds her whimsical "he he" to her message on this publicity photo. She took time to sign this at a special screening, writing her personal thoughts followed by a quick signature.

Hilary makes the cover of *Teen Magazine.* This time she uses a variation of the heart symbol above her signature and links her first name with her last name with a dramatic flair.

Buena Vista Records / Hollywood Records

HILARY DUFF

Hilary, now a rock and roll teen, simply signs this beautiful photo with her nickname, “Hil.” It was while looking at this picture and reading her kind words that I knew I wanted to share her heart with the world.

Chapter 7

Lending A Helping Hand

Hilary, always willing to lend a helping hand, asked the wardrobe department to donate a few *Lizzie* outfits to our charity. Many times the clothing had photos attached that helped verify the authenticity for the public.

Hilary is pleased to spend time visiting with a special Kids With A Cause guest before hosting the Teen Choice Awards. This magical moment (that included her dog, Lola) had both the girls smiling because Hilary said, "I think my dog likes you better than me" as Lola remained right where she was!

So at the young age of ten, what exactly did Hilary do with Kids With A Cause to lend a helping hand? Just like most of the other members of our charity, Hilary's acting career was still in the beginning stages when we met. At that time she had not had a significant lead role other than *Wendy* in *Casper meets Wendy.* It's odd to look back now (11 years later) at photos of Hilary at our charity events when she was, as she frequently reminds everyone, just a "regular kid." There were no paparazzi, no television reporters, no adoring fans and no autograph requests. She was in the public's eye, they just didn't know who she was—yet.

During the first few years of Kids With A Cause before her breakthrough role of *Lizzie McGuire*, Hilary participated in several of our programs offering a "hand-up" rather than a "hand-out" to disadvantaged youth. She always showed up on time, eager to help and attended the briefing session prior to each event.

Hilary listened carefully during the briefing sessions. She was not shy about asking questions when she was unsure of something or needed clarity about the activities or interacting with the recipients. She felt it was important to understand her responsibilities thoroughly and learn as much as she could about the kids. She often suggested ideas that enhanced our programs and were advantageous to all. She was courteous, respectful and excited to participate.

It was becoming clear to me that the young members of Kids With A Cause were taking their responsibilities seriously and frequently offering both program and fundraising suggestions. I decided to create a Youth Advisory Board and have a monthly meeting with them to obtain their input and listen to their ideas. Since there were nearly fifty members in the charity at the time, it seemed the best way to create the youth board was to have a random drawing and select ten people to serve on the Advisory Board for a six-month term. We could then select another ten members for the next term and eventually everyone would have a chance to participate and voice their ideas and offer their suggestions.

Hilary's name was selected and she served on the Youth Advisory Board in 2001, the same year she started working on *Lizzie*. The meetings were held at our office during early evening hours and there were times when Hilary would rush over directly from the set in order to attend. At one meeting she arrived with pink streaks in her hair (from the episode she was filming that day) and was very apologetic to me and the others because she didn't have time to go home first and "clean up." We were just happy she was there and that she made the effort to participate.

At the youth board meetings we had one rule for the parents—they were asked to reserve their comments and suggestions until the end of the meeting. By doing this, the kids felt empowered to voice their opinions and make their own decisions. During one meeting Susan Duff had a great idea and started to share it with the group. When Hilary and all the kids at the conference table turned around and looked at her, she remembered our "rule" and immediately apologized and said, "I'm sorry. I know it's not my turn now. How about if I just wait out in the hallway until the meeting's over and then I'll share my ideas with you, when I'm supposed to." With a big smile, she and a few of the other parents left the room so the kids could resume their open-discussion youth meeting. As eager as Susan was to help, she politely waited for the allotted time to offer her thoughts and ideas to the kids.

Hilary's commitment to Kids With A Cause was important to her and she continued to do what she could to help others. It was becoming more difficult, however, as her daily work schedule would fill up quickly and leave her little personal time to do other things she wanted to do. As the *Lizzie McGuire* series began to soar, so did the demand for Hilary. Her desire to help was abundant but her time was not, so she looked for ways that she could do something to make a difference.

While working on *Lizzie* she invited me to the set and introduced me to the other cast members as well as some of the key executives. Hilary continued to open doors and seek opportunities for our charity whenever possible. Kids With A Cause was fortunate that this was not one young Hollywood star that forgot about others as her fame was rising. She was not then, or now, a self-centered person. She always did anything and everything she could to lend a helping hand.

One day Hilary took me to the wardrobe department to see if they would be willing to donate a few items of clothing that the cast wore on the show. She knew that we could auction these *Lizzie* collectibles and raise money to provide basic necessities, such as food and clothing, to children in need. Not only did the charity receive some fabulous clothing that could be auctioned, but Hilary also asked her fellow cast members to sign their wardrobe items—knowing it would increase the value with original signatures.

Hilary also thought about Kids With A Cause when she was starring in *The Lizzie McGuire Movie*. When the filming was completed, Hilary gave me her final script that she signed as well as autographed photos of the cast. She also made arrangements so that our charity would be given tickets for the movie premiere. She knew how much it would mean for Kids With A Cause to be able to escort disadvantaged youth to this special screening. We felt lucky to have the support of this new young star and we were anxious to see her on the big screen. It was exciting for me to call a recipient organization and offer premiere tickets to the staff chaperones and young residents. Many of these children, who were now residing in a group home, had previously been abandoned, neglected and/or abused. For them to attend a movie premiere was an opportunity of a lifetime. They were thrilled to see the film but they were ecstatic about meeting this famous young star in person.

Hilary/*Lizzie* fans loved seeing their idol and the film did quite well. Billboards and movie posters went up everywhere promoting the film and her devoted fans happily stood in line to see it time and time again. In the publicity photos, Hilary was wearing a denim jacket with a striped mini skirt and tennis shoes. She decided to donate the denim jacket, seen on billboards across the country, to Kids With A Cause and help us raise funds and lend a helping hand to less fortunate children.

On the day I went to her house to pick up the now-seen-everywhere jacket, we stood in the kitchen trying to figure out where would be the best place on the jacket for her signature. We looked at the front, the inside and the back of the jacket and finally determined that the back would be a good place. She leaned on the kitchen counter with a black tip marker in her hand, signed her name and handed the jacket to me. She didn't know if someone would really buy it, but it was worth a try.

We auctioned the jacket online and the winning bid turned out to be a wonderful family in Texas (with three children) that we still communicate with to this day. They proudly framed the jacket and have it on display in their house.

On another occasion I received a call from Disney Records and they were planning a benefit concert with Hilary performing at the House of Blues in Los Angeles. They knew of Hil's ongoing involvement with Kids With A Cause and wanted the proceeds from the concert to benefit our charity. Not only were we the benefactors of this incredible performance but we also had the opportunity to invite two special guests.

The two girls I invited were big fans and were extremely excited when they heard the good news. Not only were they thrilled at the chance to see Hilary perform, but they were also going to be able to spend time with her before the concert.

When Hilary met the girls they shared memorable moments together in a private room talking, posing for pictures, laughing and having fun. During the concert that night, these special guests were not thinking about their pain—their attention was on Hilary. These adoring fans were experiencing a night of pure happiness. This was more than a wish fulfilled; it was a dream come true. They actually spent time with their favorite star who filled them with joy that would never be forgotten.

Hilary's popularity was rapidly growing with each passing day. She was on nearly every VIP guest list to attend various Hollywood events—and she always thought of Kids With A Cause and how she could help. At one event she was given a gift card from a local fast-food restaurant that was redeemable for 250 meals. She knew that this would be something that our charity could put to good use and she gave the gift card to us. With her thoughtfulness and generosity we were able to create a special Halloween costume party for kids and serve dinner, at no cost, to our guests.

Hilary was lending a helping hand because she truly cared. She was doing what made her feel good and what she wanted to do. Rarely did the public know of these acts of kindness nor did the Duffs talk about them. Hilary's grandmother used to say,

"Charity isn't charity if you have to tell people you're doing it" and Hilary believed her grandma's words. It wasn't important that it was talked about; it was important that it was done. And so she continued to offer her support in many ways and brighten the lives of kids everywhere.

It was always exciting when Susan would call and invite me to come over and pick up some of Hil's clothing. While cleaning her closets may not have been Hilary's favorite thing to do, it was great for Kids With A Cause. The clothes were always freshly laundered and packed into big bags. Susan would stand at the top of the stairs and roll the bags down to me at the bottom. We'd load them into my car and push the bags as close together as possible until they were all in and we could close the car doors. Many times I was lucky if I could still see out the back window! There were also times when Hilary would select items she thought I would like and ask me to try them on or she would put them in a bag with my name on it. She was always thinking of others—including me.

Hilary's personal clothing (that we acquired to auction) was generating additional revenue for the charity and enabling us to provide much needed support to more children. Once we were aware of the strong interest in these items, we then received some of her handbags, shoes, hats, CDs and DVDs—many with her original signature. Everybody wanted something *Hilary* but these collectible items were not always easy to find. She even donated her first prom dress and matching handbag to our charity. She was fifteen years old when she went to her first prom with a friend in

Lake Tahoe and her mom had carefully stored the elegant evening dress for her. Hilary felt good about donating the designer dress and handbag to Kids With A Cause because she knew that the money raised would help children.

More and more people began to visit our website to see what "Hilary items" we were auctioning and as a result more and more people started to learn about our charity, the kids we help and the causes we support. Hilary was helping in a much bigger way than donating some of her personal items; she was raising awareness of our philanthropic message to kids everywhere.

The number of website visitors was increasing every week as were the emails, calls and letters. It seemed that although everyone was her "Number 1 Fan", they were starting to see her not just as an actor, fashion designer or recording artist but also as a humanitarian. They were starting to see Hilary's heart. Praises, compliments and admiration were coming from kids, teens, parents and grandparents from around the world—everyone *loved* Hilary. Although she was adored as a multi-talented artist, her popularity was also increasing because of her heart and her genuine interest in others.

As her fame was exploding worldwide, a well-known and respected wish granting organization contacted Kids With A Cause about Hilary. Many young children were waiting for their one special wish to be granted and that wish was to meet Hilary. This was quite amazing to hear because these children, facing life threatening or life altering illnesses, could have wished for anything including a trip to Paris or a day at Disneyland or a chance to swim with dolphins—but what they wanted more than anything else was to meet their favorite person in the world: Hilary Duff.

The first wish request Kids With A Cause and Hilary fulfilled was in San Diego during Hil's first concert tour. After coordinating the logistics with the wish organization and the Duffs, I was excited to meet the little girl whose dream was about to come true. I packed a big gift bag for her filled with some of Hilary's personal clothing, various items from *Stuff by Hilary Duff*, the new Hilary CD, posters, headshots and lots more.

I met the child and her mom near the box office in front of the music venue. I explained that we would be meeting Hilary in a private area in a few minutes. In the meantime, I began to show the little girl the gifts I brought for her. As I was showing her each item, I could feel, or sense, that we were not alone. I suddenly looked up and noticed a group of people surrounding us. They were all looking to see what was going on and the crowd was growing quickly. The next thing I knew there was a lot of commotion and then I heard a woman tell her child, "Go over to that lady and ask her for something. She's giving away some things of Hilary's." As the crowd continued to grow and become more intense, the security guards showed up just in time to escort us inside to meet Hilary. From that day on I always waited to give the gifts to our special guests once we were *inside* the Meet & Greet room.

We then entered a small room and waited for Hilary. I explained to the little girl that Hilary was in her dressing room getting ready for her concert. I reassured her that Hilary knew we were there and that soon she would be coming into our private room before she went on stage to perform. This little girl was so excited she could hardly wait.

When the doors opened and Hilary walked in, all I could see were big smiles as they greeted each other with heartfelt hugs. I could tell that this moment meant a lot to both the girls (as well as their moms who were watching it all) and they spent time together talking and taking pictures. Hilary signed the CD that I had in the gift bag as well as some of the photos. This meeting was an extra special one because Haylie was there, too, and the three girls sat together and had a good time just hanging out before "show time."

The fulfillment of this first wish was one I will never forget and the memorable day this young fan experienced was beyond words. I sat next to her at the concert and watched as she sweetly sang every word to every song. I also watched her family and could clearly see how much this special day meant to them. They were very appreciative and couldn't thank me enough, but their tears of joy said it all. This little girl's dream came true and it was the beginning of my wonderful role to work with the Duffs and continue to grant many more wishes in the future.

The word started to spread about these special wish granting situations and our office began to receive requests from around the world. We could not possibly handle (nor could Hilary meet) all of the individuals who now were requesting this once-in-a-lifetime opportunity. We needed to establish procedures and policies that would enable Kids With A Cause to work directly with the coordinators of non-profit wish granting organizations. We agreed to give concert tickets to the immediate family members so the entire family could enjoy the performance together. Due to the small size of the meeting areas, as well as Hilary's time limitation prior to her show, Meet & Greet passes were given to the child and parents only.

By the time Hilary's second tour began we had our plans in place and hundreds of children had their wishes granted. Each time, Kids With A Cause would send a gift box full of "Hilary items" a few weeks after the concert with a card letting the child know that we were thinking of him or her and sending our best wishes. It was our hope that meeting Hilary and watching her perform would be an experience they would never forget and we wanted those special memories to linger even longer.

The gift boxes were never expected and always received with surprise and delight. As I was sending these gifts to the children, there were many times that flowers or gifts were sent to me. These thoughtful gifts, sent from the parents, included beautiful thank you cards letting me know how much this meant to them and their child and expressing their sincere gratitude and appreciation for coordinating this unforgettable opportunity. Most people were surprised that Hilary would actually take the time to meet with her fans before her concert performance, but even more surprised (and thrilled) to see her beautiful smile and watch her greet each guest with genuine warmth and sincerity.

In addition to providing Meet & Greet passes and concert tickets for these special guests, Susan and Hilary realized the additional time this required and wanted Kids With A Cause to benefit, too. They knew that numerous hours were spent each week coordinating and fulfilling these important wishes. They decided that a small percentage of every ticket sale would be donated to our organization to further our mission and continue our charitable work. When Susan explained this contribution concept to me, I had no idea that Hilary would be performing in nearly every major city in the U.S. to sell-out crowds. This ongoing support enabled our organization to extend its programs and services to more children everywhere. Once again, it was another example of Hilary and her heart.

Concerts, clothing, auction items and wish requests weren't the only ways that Hilary continued to lend a helping hand. She also made sure that Kids With A Cause was able to escort disadvantaged youth to her movie premieres and after-parties including *A Cinderella Story*, *Raise Your Voice* and *A Perfect Man*. At each one of these special occasions it was not only the movie that put smiles on the children's faces, but the chance to meet Hilary. As usual, she spent time with our guests and showed them how much it meant to her that they were there and how special they were to her.

One special guest was lucky enough to attend the Teen Choice Awards that Hilary hosted. Not only was this teenage girl invited to go to the show (with great seats near the stage) but I was also able to take her back stage to Hilary's dressing room. This created a wonderful opportunity for the girls to spend some time together in a private setting and talk. Even Hilary's dog, Lola, was there and photos were taken of all of them. This young teen was so overwhelmed when she actually met her idol that as we left the dressing room she started to cry. She reminded me that these were "happy tears" and I ran back in to grab a tissue for her. Then, of course, she didn't want to throw the tissue away—because it came from Hilary's dressing room!

The night turned out to be fantastic and I spent time with the young girl and her mother the next day, too. This gracious, and very appreciative teen, told me that she was barely able to sleep because she kept thinking about the amazing experience she had and was re-living it over and over again in her mind until she finally fell asleep in the early hours of the morning.

There were also numerous requests for phone calls from Hilary. This was not easy, especially if she was traveling and there was a vast difference in time zones. She did, however, try to arrange her schedule (even if it meant getting up before sunrise) to call the kids who were too ill to travel and meet her personally. I would help coordinate the call time and tell Hilary a little about the individual prior to her making the call. I hoped this would help the conversation go smoothly and be somewhat easier for both of them since they didn't know each other and could not meet face to face. Every time, without fail, the parents would call me afterwards to let me know how much this meant to their child and would thank me over and over again. It really wasn't me; it was Hilary. She was a bright light to these kids even during their darkest hours.

Her licensing company was also willing to help and generously donated Hilary's products including cosmetics, clothing, hair dryers, curling irons, bedding, pillows, calendars, backpacks, school supplies and much more. These "Hilary items" were carefully wrapped and included in the gift boxes that Kids With A Cause would send to our special friends after they met Hilary or spoke with her on the phone. Although it might seem like a small gesture, we were often told that the surprise gift box helped in more ways than we could image. Many times these valued gifts helped keep dreams alive and gave these children a reason to smile during difficult times.

When her own clothing line *Stuff by Hilary Duff* was launched, she donated hundreds of sample items to Kids With A Cause. Since these items were production samples and had not been released to the retailers yet, they could not be sold to the general public. To prevent the sale of these items it was required that each garment had a cut in the fabric. I have seen many production samples from other manufacturers and sometimes the cuts have been so large that the clothing was un-wearable. With Hilary's samples I would often times have to hold them up to the light to find the cut because it was so small and barely noticeable. These sample items have been treasured by children around the world including tsunami survivors in India, orphan children in Mexico and Fiji, tornado, fire and flood victims in the United States as well as children in hospitals, homeless shelters and foster homes.

Hilary and Susan were also very responsive when Kids With A Cause would receive a call about "rush" wishes (usually a terminal situation with little time left). One day I was in the office when I received a call regarding a rush wish request to meet Hilary. I wasn't sure what, if anything, we could do so I called Susan. Hilary happened to be filming a commercial with Haylie that day and Susan made arrangements for me to escort the child and her family on the set to meet the girls. It turned out to be one of the best wishes ever fulfilled as this young girl was able to spend the entire day on the set, visit with Hilary and Haylie in their production trailer, have lunch with them and, of course, watch the filming of the commercial sitting in a director's chair.

Hilary's helping hands were never idle. She was always willing to do what she could when she could. She knew, as she had told me years ago when we were visiting children in the hospital, "That could be me" and she wanted to do whatever she could to lift their spirits, show her support and encourage them to be brave, strong and optimistic.

Chapter 8

Special Moments And Special Memories

There were many surprises for Hilary at her Sweet Sixteen Celebration. Her enthusiasm and excitement are seen by all as a Kids With A Cause performer sings *Sixteen Candles* to her and invites her to the dance floor.

Hilary collects sixteen crystal roses from her guests to create an everlasting bouquet during her birthday celebration. Her expression shows how happy she is and how much it means to celebrate this special day with special guests.

It seemed that no matter what Hilary did it turned into a special moment. With her unique charm and a smile that could light up a room, she continued to melt the hearts of people everywhere. She was courteous and gracious and always appreciative of the support from her fans. There were many times she would tell me how incredibly lucky she felt to be in a position that was allowing her the opportunity and ability to affect so many people's lives.

And she wasn't just affecting the lives of kids and teenagers. Parents and grandparents were fans, too, and had respect and admiration for this young star that was rocking the world. Parents were proud that their children chose Hilary as their role model and looked up to her because of *who* she was. Her image was wholesome and refreshing. Her songs were positive and encouraging, especially to kids experiencing the common yet challenging aspects of growing up. Through her music Hilary passionately delivered powerful messages to young and impressionable audiences everywhere. Her songs were insightful, inspirational and motivational to people of all ages.

Some of the fans that attended her concerts were very young and chaperoned by their parents. For many of these young fans this was their first concert—but they came prepared. They took time to design posters and create signs with messages to Hilary, that they enthusiastically held throughout the concert, to express their feelings for her. There was pink colored clothing as far as the eye could see (since pink was Hilary's favorite color at the time) along with tons of fans wearing *Stuff by Hilary Duff* outfits. Susan and I would stand by the stage and look out at the enormous crowds to see not just young fans but their entire families, too. It sometimes seemed hard for us to believe that Hilary was attracting the thousands and thousands of fans that showed up in every city on her tour. Not that we didn't believe in her talent or ability, it was just somewhat overwhelming to see these huge crowds and know that her fan base was growing so rapidly. She had definitely become an A-List celebrity that was sought after by every media outlet conceivable.

For many of these fans seeing Hilary on stage was a memory of a lifetime. For many others capturing a small piece of memorabilia from the evening was icing on the cake. I remember watching the confetti machines shoot glimmering streams of colored foil into the air during her closing song and hearing her fans scream and applaud for an encore. When the concert ended and the lights came up, announcements were made asking people to exit. Kids and teens would rush down to the floor and scramble to pick up any scrap of confetti they could find. These were not just colorful pieces of confetti; they were important keepsake souvenirs to her adoring fans.

It was amazing to see the impact Hilary had on people everywhere. She was touching the lives and the hearts of millions and leaving positive and lasting impressions with them. There are hundreds of special moments and special memories I have and each one is just as meaningful as the next. It would take volumes to write about every child, every circumstance, every smile and yet I feel compelled to write about a few special memories that reveal the true, and untold, heart of Hilary.

Let me start with Emily. Kids With A Cause was planning a hospital visit to brighten the day for the pediatric patients. As usual, we had fun activities planned and gifts for each patient. Most of our activities are conducted in a playroom or play area within the hospital but not all patients feel well enough to attend and participate. It has always been important to Kids With A Cause to allot additional time and conduct personal in-room visits for those unable to join us for the group activities.

During these special personal visits there is always someone on the nursing staff who escorts us and asks each patient's permission for us to visit before we enter the room. The hospital personnel also tells us the patient's name and age and informs us of any restrictions or limitations that may be important for us to know. It was during our in-room visits that we had the pleasure of meeting Emily.

Initially when Emily heard about our plans to visit her, she told the nurse she didn't feel up to having visitors so we were prepared to leave her gifts at the nursing station. While we were selecting the gifts we thought she would enjoy, Emily changed her mind and decided that it might be fun to see us after all. As we entered the room she sat up in her bed and seemed quite curious about who we were and why we were there. Her mother sat by her bedside and listened as we introduced ourselves.

Within a few minutes, Emily began to share many stories about her young nine-year-old life with us. She told us about her surgeries, her hobbies and interests, her family and her dog. As we spent time with her we learned that much of her life had been spent in a hospital and that she had already had over 48 surgeries! Emily was not able to attend school on a regular basis because of the many complications of her illness. She was, however, just like any other little girl and longed to have friends to talk with and share good times. Kids With A Cause members became the friends that Emily wanted.

We listened and talked and gave her the gifts we brought including a new Barbie doll, a few Disney CDs and some art & craft projects. We stayed in her hospital room much longer than we expected (she had captured our hearts by this time) and helped her dress and undress Barbie over and over again with all the new outfits we gave her. She drew pictures for us with her new colorful markers and talked and talked and *talked.* Even though our program went far beyond the scheduled time, it was difficult to say goodbye to this sweet little girl. Her mom tried to help and explained to Emily that it was time for us to go and then looked at us and said, "Emily loves to talk and doesn't like to say goodbye." On this day, neither did we.

Emily was experiencing a very challenging health situation and the only answer for her future well being meant a big surgery—a SIX-ORGAN transplant. Although she was on the transplant waiting list, the organ donor had to be a perfect match in order for this difficult and delicate surgery to have successful results.

During what seemed to be an endless waiting period, Emily remained hospitalized and was monitored every hour throughout the day and night. She was connected to machines that would feed her, provide her with pain medication, keep her blood levels stable and help keep her alive with hope for a brighter tomorrow. Several members of Kids With A Cause, as well as our staff, made frequent visits to see Emily and help keep her spirits up during this difficult time of uncertainty.

It was during one of my evening visits with Emily that she told me she was having trouble sleeping at night. She said she had nightmares that would scare her and wake her up and then she couldn't go back to sleep again. She was sure if she had a Hilary Duff comforter and pillow it would make her "feel happy" and then, hopefully, the nightmares would go away. Emily's mother wanted to buy the Hilary Duff bedding for her daughter but had no luck. These items were now discontinued and there wasn't a store around that could help.

When I told Susan Duff about this young child's request, Susan immediately called the licensing company and inquired about any items, even samples, that might still be around. It didn't surprise me when Susan called me later that day and told me the bedding would be delivered to my office. It was such a great feeling to take the much-desired comforter and pillow, along with a string of Hilary nightlights, to Emily and see the expression on her face. She was so overjoyed that she couldn't stop hugging me for what seemed to be several minutes. I think it was the longest lasting hug I have ever gotten from anyone—thanks, once again, to the kindness of the Duffs. The next day Emily called to tell me that she didn't have any nightmares that night and she was sure it was because of Hilary's comforter, pillow and nightlights.

After five long months of waiting, Emily's mother finally received the call they had been waiting for during the early morning hours on September 25th (three days before Hilary's birthday). It was now time for Emily, age eleven, to have her "big surgery" and receive the vital organs she needed. Although a six-organ transplant came with high risks and unknown outcomes, I am thrilled to say that Emily recently celebrated her third anniversary of this amazing surgery. She is strong, courageous, bright, caring and loving and will always be a friend to all of us at Kids With A Cause. She is our "miracle girl."

There was another time that Hilary and Susan helped make Kids With A Cause look like a hero. There was a young girl with cerebral palsy who was sure that she, along with thousands of others with the same belief, was Hilary's "Number 1 Fan." She had seen every episode of *Lizzie*, watched all of Hilary's movies, owned all of Hilary's CDs, read every magazine about Hilary and couldn't get enough of her favorite teen idol. This young fan followed everything about Hilary and knew her rock star favorite would soon be performing in a city near her. She was thrilled to find out that her aunt would be escorting her to the concert and soon she would be able to experience the sights and sounds of Hilary. What she didn't know was that one of the television entertainment shows had contacted Kids With A Cause and had plans to find and reveal that illusive "Number 1 Fan."

The show producers were hard at work trying to determine who *was* the "Number 1 Fan." Their plans were to identify this individual and capture a surprise backstage meeting with Hilary. I received a call about the show because the producers knew of Hilary's involvement with our charity. They wanted to add to the surprise and include one special Kids With A Cause guest, too. I knew, without a doubt, who would be perfect for this special "Number 1 Fan" backstage meeting—Kady.

Since this was going to be a surprise meeting, I couldn't call Kady and tell her anything. I would wait until she was in school and then call her grandmother to discuss the details. Kady was living with her grandparents and I knew they wanted the best for Kady and this would be the surprise of a lifetime—that is if we could all keep it a secret. And we did. For several weeks I sent emails with concert information and updates. We all knew what was about to happen, except Kady. She had no idea that soon she would be experiencing far more than attending the concert of her dreams; she was actually going to be meeting Hilary.

On the day of the concert and television taping, I arrived at the venue, parked my car, tucked the treasured Hilary gift bag under my arm and went to find the Duffs. The assistant tour manager knew about Kady's surprise and was ready to escort us backstage. The plan was for me to receive a call from Kady's aunt (pretending she was speaking to someone else to make sure we kept the surprise) so that we could determine a place to meet each other.

It all happened just as we had hoped and I could see Kady's wheelchair getting closer to where I was waiting to surprise her. I suddenly stepped in front of her with a big smile. She excitedly screamed when she saw me, since she had no idea that I was going to be there. I could only imagine what was going to happen when she would soon learn that she was actually going to be meeting her favorite star of all time.

It was great to see Kady and we talked and talked as her aunt pushed the wheelchair closer and closer to the reserved meeting room backstage. Kady was so consumed with conversation that she was not paying attention to anything around her (including where we were going) and her excitement about being together and going to Hilary's concert intensified with each passing minute. Suddenly doors opened and we entered a small private room where she immediately spotted Susan. I introduced Kady to Susan and they hugged each other. Susan welcomed her with open arms and an open heart and sat with her until the big surprise was revealed. This time when the doors opened, Hilary walked into the room.

Kady was so shocked when she saw Hilary that she started to cry. She turned to me with tears streaming down her face and said, "Please tell me this is real and that I'm not dreaming." Hilary and Kady spent time together and Hil autographed a pair of jeans from her personal wardrobe that I had included in the gift bag. They took photos together and hugged right before Hilary went on stage. This was an unforgettable moment and memory for all of us, but especially for Kady.

And as special as special can get, Hilary's Sweet Sixteen birthday celebration gave me an opportunity to meet sweet Renee. This young lady is truly an angel, only one with muscular dystrophy who uses a motorized wheelchair as her wings. Renee was one of the guests attending a special Kids With A Cause event that was created to pay tribute to Hilary and her soon-to-be sixteenth birthday. This *Birthday With A Cause,* however, was more than a celebration of this milestone birthday for Hilary; it was a time to honor special guests with special needs and give them an opportunity to share this spectacular day with their favorite teen star.

As the word spread about this incredible opportunity corporations and individuals purchased tickets to sponsor children and teens with various challenges and illnesses. These special guests waited with excitement for the day to finally arrive. They could not believe their eyes when the doors opened and they were escorted into a luxurious hotel ballroom for this intimate and private party for Hilary. It was the thrill of a lifetime for these young guests to get dressed up, go to an elegant hotel and most importantly, have the chance to meet Hilary and celebrate her sixteenth birthday with her.

The room was decorated beautifully with floral arrangements and fine china place settings on each of the linen-covered tables. In front of the ballroom, for all to see, was a banquet table for Hilary, Haylie and sixteen other close friends who joined her. A large pink and white banner printed with the words *"Happy Birthday, Hilary"* was draped behind the banquet table and classical music was playing in the background. The graceful feel of the room was prominent and the impressive setting made the guests feel very special, almost as if they were royalty. As Hilary entered the room she was greeted with smiles and applause from all in attendance.

The program began with beautiful musical performances dedicated to Hilary, by Kids With A Cause members, and she watched and listened intently with appreciation and admiration of her talented peers. Next it was my turn to welcome everyone, especially Hilary, and I spoke about the importance of this day. Although the celebration was in her honor I knew it meant a lot to her to share this memorable occasion with special guests. I talked about Hilary's wonderful attributes and expressed the pleasure I have had over the years of watching her grow into a dignified young lady with a heart of gold.

During the birthday celebration each guest was given an opportunity to meet and visit with Hilary and have a keepsake photo taken with her. After everyone had a chance to spend time with this young and beautiful star it was now time for her birthday cake. The cake was one of her favorites—strawberry with butter cream frosting. When the candles were lit, her family gathered around her and everyone sang *Happy Birthday*. Hilary then thought carefully for a few seconds, made a wish and blew out all the candles. As the guests were enjoying their cake, Hilary went to every table to personally thank each person for coming to her birthday celebration. She shook hands with everyone including the parents, grandparents, caregivers, siblings and friends and expressed her appreciation to them for taking the time to share this special day with her.

Just before the cake presentation, I had given sixteen pink crystal roses to sixteen guests in the room. They were each to give their rose to Hilary and help her create a birthday bouquet that would last forever. While doing this one of the individuals I was drawn towards was Renee. I don't know if it was her dark brown eyes and beautiful hair that struck me or if it was her delightful dimples that I saw when she smiled. Whatever it was, I went over to talk with her and handed her one of the pink roses to give to Hilary.

Renee was a teenager at the time and would soon be turning sixteen, too. Although she was quite thin in stature, I could sense she was a strong and determined young lady. She was positive and upbeat and, as I quickly learned, a person with no self pity. I knew I liked her the moment I met her. Renee handed Hilary the crystal rose to add to the birthday bouquet and they exchanged smiles and hugs and spoke for a while. Before I knew it, Renee had met the entire Duff family, the hotel staff, the event support team and the Kids With A Cause performers. She certainly knew how to charm everyone and work a room.

My friendship continued with Renee as it does to this day. She and I have worked together on various projects and she currently serves as the Kids With A

Cause Special Correspondent. She helps our charity by writing articles for our website and provides support in any way she can. She does not let something like a disability or the fact that she is confined to a wheelchair hold her back. She believes that we all can help one another and she is an outstanding example for others to follow. There are many days that I feel this special angel came into my life to inspire me and to encourage me to continue on the path of my philanthropic journey.

Another huge Hilary fan was Tori. In fact, according to Tori, she was Hilary's "Number 1 Fan." Her bedroom walls were covered with Hilary posters, she owned all of Hilary's CDs and movies, she had a wardrobe of *Stuff by Hilary Duff* clothing and each night she would fall asleep happily tucked into her Hilary Duff sheets.

We all know how important birthdays can be to a young child and little Tori was no different than any other child in that respect. This birthday was going to be the best one ever and Tori could hardly wait. She was counting the days and getting more excited as the date drew closer. She was thrilled that she was going to be celebrating her seventh birthday seeing her favorite teen star, Hilary Duff, in concert—at least that's what she thought.

Days before the concert Tori and her mom went shopping to select just the right outfit to wear to this once-in-a-lifetime occasion. This was Tori's first concert and her mother was overjoyed knowing that her daughter's dream was about to come true. Since Tori has spina bifida and needs a wheelchair for her mobility, her mom wanted to be certain that her daughter's ticket was in an accessible seating area. She called the venue and that's when the bad news followed.

Tori did have one ticket that was in accessible seating but this particular venue did not provide a chaperone pass, which is customarily given for a wheelchair attendant. This meant there was no ticket for Tori's mother to accompany her young daughter. Her mom, surprised to learn of this, explained that Tori was only seven years old, in a wheelchair and could not possibly go alone. She willing offered to purchase a ticket for herself but was told that it was a sold-out concert and there were no tickets available. Tori's mother clarified that she did not need a seat and offered to stand behind her daughter's wheelchair. She couldn't believe her ears when she heard the reservation agent tell her, "I'm very sorry but everyone needs a ticket. There are no extra tickets and there's nothing I can do." Tori's mom felt her heart sink in her chest.

News traveled quickly about the story of Tori, so much so that it was the lead story on several primetime news programs that night. Once again, the next day the phone started to ring in our office with requests for Kids With A Cause to help. I listened to the heartbreaking story from several individuals and did what I normally did—called the Duffs. When I told them about this little girl and explained why she would not be able to celebrate her birthday as she had wished at Hilary's concert, Susan made sure that Tori and her entire family had front row tickets.

I, of course, got to be the lucky one and respond to the now widely spread public plea for a ticket. One of the news reporters covering the story asked permission to broadcast me talking with Tori on the phone and giving her the great news. Tori attentively listened to every word I was saying and I could almost hear her holding her breath in anticipation when I told her I had spoken to the Duff family about the extra ticket her mother needed. When I explained that Hilary wanted Tori and her entire family to go to the concert and sit in the front row, she started to cry. The next day I watched the news coverage of the special message I delivered to Tori and saw her wipe away tears she could not hold back. I knew they were happy tears and, once again, it was the Duffs doing what they could to make this little girl's dream come true.

The night of the concert came and I was anxiously waiting to meet Tori with my usual Hilary gift bag. This young child was so delightful and the family could not have been nicer and more appreciative of the kind gesture of the Duffs and our charity. I took Tori and her mom backstage to meet Hilary before the magical night unfolded.

Tori and her family were then escorted to the front row and chairs were removed to allow enough room for the wheelchair. When the family was settled in their seats and I saw the big smile on Tori's face, I went to thank Susan for giving this little girl the happiest birthday ever. Susan then took me to one of the merchandise booths and gave me one of Hilary's pink hoodies to give to Tori. She said, "You don't have to tell her where it came from, just give it to her."

And so I did. At this point, Tori's mom stood up, tears in her eyes and hugged me. She couldn't believe the generosity and kindness that was extended to her daughter and her family and felt she would never be able to thank us enough for all that we had done. It's moment and memories like these that will stay with me forever.

There were also many children, healthy and strong, who sadly were experiencing the pain and difficulty of losing a sibling or parent. Several caring and loving support groups contacted Kids With A Cause to see if there was anything we could do to brighten the lives of these young children during their grieving process. It seemed to me that going to the movies with friends, especially if the films featured their favorite stars, could be uplifting and bring pleasure to these kids, even if for a while. When the release date for *A Cinderella Story* was announced I thought it might be a good idea to have a special screening especially for the children in these bereavement groups.

Hilary was very willing to participate and suggested that we also invite Dan Byrd, one of her co-stars in the film, to see if he might want to join her, too. This premiere event required a tremendous amount of time, energy and effort because it was important to make it a unique and memorable experience for the group of children attending. I contacted Dan and he eagerly agreed to join Hilary, as did Haylie. I knew with Hilary, Haylie and Dan we had a great start and now I needed to work out several other details, such as locating a theater that would donate the space, determining if there would be time for a Meet & Greet, obtaining snacks and beverages for the kids and coordinating many other details, such as security and transportation, in order to make it all work.

The theater manager I approached with this somewhat-out-of-the-ordinary request was a young father and a fantastic person. Not only did he agree to donate the theater space but he was also willing to provide popcorn, snacks and soft drinks for all the guests. Although I felt I was off to a good start with permission to view the film and a cooperative theater manager, there were many more steps to go.

The next big item was the *Cinderella* dress. I thought it would be great for this young audience to see Hilary in the beautiful white gown she actually wore in the film. After discussing this possibility with the studio executives, it was agreed that the formal gown would be ready for Hilary to wear that day. They then provided Hilary with the dress measurements (since the filming took place several months earlier and Hilary's size may have changed), only to find that alterations were, in fact, necessary. Hilary was assured that the dress would fit her perfectly.

Hilary arrived on the day of the special premiere and began to get ready. When she slipped on the dress she was shocked to find that it was nearly three inches too big for her. The gown had been dry cleaned and altered as promised, but not to Hilary's measurements. When she called to tell me what had happened, the only thing we could do at this point was to find someone with a *lot* of safety pins to adjust the floor length dress to fit her. The public never knew about any of this and Hilary's arrival in this magnificent dress was a breath-taking moment of beauty and splendor.

The next challenge was the car. It seemed that *Cinderella* should arrive in something other than a modern day limo so I researched and located the car that was used in the film. The owner lived near the theater (lucky me) and was willing to drive Hilary, Haylie and Dan on the back of his Ford Mustang convertible to the red carpet for their grand arrival. The only problem, which I hadn't thought about, was—the weather. It turned out to be a windy day and driving on the freeway in a convertible didn't help matters. Hilary, in keeping with the *Cinderella* theme had her hair pulled back from her face with long, beautiful curls flowing past her shoulders and down her back. As she was riding in the convertible she was desperately fighting the wind and trying to keep her elegant hairstyle in place. She held her hands close to her head during the entire drive to the theater and then stopped for a quick touch up right before the car turned the final corner and she was in full view of her fans.

So now that her gown was safety-pinned to fit her and her curls were smooth and in place she was ready to meet her guests. The crowd was gathering and moving as close to the red carpet as they could possibly get with their cameras ready. When the convertible began its approach to the theater entrance and Hilary was spotted, the screams and cheers were deafening. She looked absolutely gorgeous as she gracefully put her hand in Dan's and stepped out of the car to greet her fans.

As she walked the red carpet to enter the theater she stopped to shake hands, sign autographs and pose for pictures along the way. She looked like a princess that stepped out of a fairy tale book and smiled and waved to all. With Dan and Haylie right behind her, the excitement soared as the magical event was about to begin.

Each guest received a laminated *All Access* pass that had a photo of Hilary in the identical ballgown she wore in the film and was wearing that day. These VIP passes were valued credentials that provided entrance inside the theater to a small private room set up for photos. In the background was *A Cinderella Story* movie poster and Hilary, Haylie and Dan happily greeted each guest as pictures were taken to capture this unforgettable moment. Although the guests were excited to see the movie I think they were more excited to meet Hilary and have their picture taken with her. Each guest then received a gift bag with treasured souvenirs including tiaras, *Zorro* masks, *Cinderella* body glitter, lip-gloss as well as Hilary Duff sun glasses, charm bracelets, CDs, t-shirts and more. As they entered the theater to select their seats, they all had their snacks, keepsake photos, gift bags and big smiles.

Meeting Hilary, Haylie and Dan was just the beginning of this magical and memorable day. As the lights dimmed and the movie began all I could hear was thunderous applause and ear piercing whistles from a theater packed with cheering fans. Everyone loved the movie and as a special treat at the end of the screening one of the producers joined the cast on stage to share some funny and interesting behind-the-scenes stories. A short clip of the movie's "bloopers" was shown and the cast discussed their favorite scenes, funny scenes, difficult scenes and other inside secrets about filming the movie.

There was also time for the audience to ask the cast and producer questions about the film, the wardrobe, the audition process, the actors or the entertainment industry in general. I am quite sure that the audience could have stayed and asked questions all day but Hilary had a plane to catch and had to say her goodbyes and dash out the door. Even after she left, the excitement lingered. It was great to see kids, who were struggling with the loss of a family member, experience happiness and joy again and feel like they were on top of the world. And for that day, they probably felt like they were.

There are many other children whose lives drastically change in just a matter of minutes. The young survivors of hurricanes, tornadoes, earthquakes, fires, floods or other natural disasters often feel they may never smile again. For many, it is not only the loss of their homes, pets and personal possessions but also the realization that their lives have been drastically changed and will never be the same as before. To experience such life changing and devastating hardships can be very unsettling, particularly to children, and Kids With A Cause steps in to provide assistance, comfort and support whenever possible.

The day of the terrible tsunami, December 26, 2004, (just one day after the joyous celebration of Christmas) I happened to be in my office. I thought it would be a good time to get caught up on some of my work and assumed it would be a quiet day. Suddenly, the phone started to ring (all three lines lit up at once) and people began telling me about the tsunami, describing the horrible situation and expressing their concerns for the lives of thousands of people affected by this enormous swell of destruction. Since I didn't have a television in the office, I decided to take my work home, turn on the news and find out more. Most of the people calling, including many Kids With A Cause members, wanted to know what our charity could do to help the unfortunate individuals whose lives were now shattered.

I, as millions of others around the world, watched in disbelief at the massive loss of lives and inconceivable widespread damage. Initially I felt helpless, especially living so far away. It seemed at the time there was very little our charity could do to help. The larger well-established emergency relief organizations immediately reacted and set up donation campaigns and large sums of money were accumulating quickly. People everywhere wanted to help in any way possible.

I decided it would be beneficial to call the Kids With A Cause youth members together and obtain their input before determining what we should do and the steps we would need to take. It was always important to me to include the kids and listen to their ideas and suggestions before developing program plans. The kids provided me with a refreshing insight, a youthful view, of what they felt would be important to kids their age. It was up to me then to create a program that would meet the kids' objectives and provide the needed assistance.

As each day passed more and more money was attained from all parts of the world due to many generous donors and successful global fundraising efforts. This strong financial stream of support indicated that securing money for urgent emergency relief was not an overwhelming problem without a solution. The focus now began to slowly expand and include not only immediate survival supplies but also long-term necessities in anticipation of the needs in the upcoming months and years ahead. As more facts about the tsunami destruction were revealed, more needs became apparent as well.

Nearly one-third of the dead were children. Thousands were separated from their families and were unsure of the fate of their parents or the whereabouts of their relatives. Over one thousand schools across the region were damaged or completely destroyed, suddenly leaving children without their important daily educational routine or a place to learn. Children were struggling to cope with their grief, fear and uncertainty of their future.

Following a crisis, going back to school is one of the first steps in a child's recovery and Kids With A Cause decided to help, even if in a small way, with this critical educational endeavor. We created a Tsunami Relief Fund and developed several fundraising programs and activities to secure contributions for this important cause. All donations were deposited in the bank until we could determine the best possible way to provide this desperately needed educational support. Since we knew that the larger organizations were providing immediate emergency assistance and fulfilling basic survival needs, Kids With A Cause decided to initiate a fundraising campaign directed at the educational needs of the young students.

After researching various areas affected by the tsunami we located a region in Chennai, India, with a school that provided education to the "poorest of the poor." It was called St. Thomas Free Primary School and it was exactly that—free to nearly 1,200 children. All of the students lived with their families in the "slums" nearby and for most of these young children the only meal of the day was their school lunch.

Their small thatch and tin roofed huts that once stood side by side along the coast were completely destroyed and thousands of people ran through the flooding waters to find safety somewhere. Next to the primary school was St. Thomas Cathedral that miraculously remained standing. The church opened its doors and provided shelter for thousands of survivors. Kids With A Cause decided to help the children in this very poor area in India and wanted to do all that we could to help rebuild the heavily damaged school.

Hilary was on tour in Canada when she heard of the devastating news and wanted to do something, too. She knew Kids With A Cause was creating a campaign to raise funds for the school project and she was determined to join our efforts and help in any way she could. It was a wonderful surprise for me to learn that she had decided to have a benefit concert and donate 100% of the concert proceeds to the Kids With A Cause Tsunami Relief Fund. She felt good knowing that she could help and was happy to contribute to the rebuilding of the school. Just as in the past, Hilary continued to do what she could to help and, at this point, I was now convinced she was part angel and an answer to the prayers of many people.

I was there the night of the benefit concert escorting Kids With A Cause special guests. As soon as the final encore ended, Susan called my cell phone. She wanted me to meet Hilary on the tour bus because Hil "had something she wanted to give me." Never did I expect what was about to happen. As I entered the bus and greeted the band and members of Hilary's tour entourage, I saw Susan who was grinning from ear to ear. She told Hil that I was there and then invited me back to Hilary's room at the back of the bus.

Hilary had her shoes off and was flopped down on her bed after an exhausting performance but quickly got up to hug me. She then handed me an envelope and said, "Here, this is for you—open it." So I did. I could hardly believe my eyes when I tore open the envelope and saw the check she was donating for the school project in India. I was shocked at the amount she eagerly and generously contributed, but I shouldn't have been. That's who Hilary is—a genuinely caring and compassionate human being. We hugged again and I left overwhelmed and speechless. There were just no words to thank her enough.

Because of this incredible and thoughtful donation, today there is a new St. Thomas Free

Primary School in Chennai, India. This four-story building has tile floors, instead of dirt, and an area outside for the children to play. It is our hope to continue to help these deserving young students and provide them with desks, school supplies and even a computer lab to help them pursue their educational dreams.

There are hundreds of special moments and special memories that Hilary has created for others. She does it without needing or wanting publicity but purely because of her caring heart. She once thanked me for “being such a great role model,” but I think I’m the one who should be thanking her.

Chapter 9

It's Not Always Easy To Understand

Hilary warms the heart of a young fan and "makes his day." From the look on Hil's face, it seems like he's capturing a piece of her heart, too!

Hilary spends an "up close and personal" moment with a special guest during a Kids With A Cause hospital visit. These precious memories mean more than can be imagined.

Why is it that some children are faced with health challenges and find that routine every day tasks (at least for most) can be time consuming, difficult or impossible for them? Why do children live in parts of the world without clean water to drink or enough food to eat? Why are children born with birth defects or suffer from severe injuries? Why are they exposed to weapons and war and HIV/AIDS? I'm not sure anyone has precise answers to these questions or convincing explanations. It's not easy for anyone to understand and it wasn't easy for Hilary.

Seeing children who are forced to face life differently can stir many emotions and create mixed feelings. While our heart may break to see them in pain or unable to run and play, we may feel encouraged or inspired by their sometimes almost miraculous accomplishments. They are often times, and rightly so, referred to as courageous, brave, champions or even heroes.

Not many people feel comfortable or know how to handle the all-too-common situation of facing others who are different, especially when it involves children. Do we feel sorry for them? Do we ignore them? Or do we pretend we just don't see the difference? Kids With A Cause members learn to see these kids not as *different* but simply kids that do things *differently*.

It has always been important to me to open the doors of communication and gain knowledge. The best way to learn about differences is to talk about them and to ask questions. Many people are concerned about asking the wrong question or saying something inappropriate and, as a result, they shy away from any conversation to avoid a potentially awkward situation. I have found from working with kids with differences that what they want more than anything is to be treated like "normal kids." They do not like to be stared at or ignored. Knowing this, it was important for Kids With A Cause members to talk with kids who do things differently and learn. Over the years we have received countless compliments about how comfortable our youth members are with children with challenges and how well they interact with them.

There are times when a difference can be quite noticeable and other times when it is almost invisible. We have met children with cystic fibrosis, epilepsy, heart problems and many other illnesses or conditions where their physical appearance seems to be healthy. They participate in what they can, when they can and may only have limitations or restrictions when specific activities become problematic for them. There are also times when a child begins life healthy and is later diagnosed with a life-threatening illness, as in the case of Hope.

Hope, twelve years old, lived with her mother, father and two older sisters. She was a tall, beautiful redhead full of energy and involved in basketball and cheerleading and many other sport and recreational activities. One day Hope's right knee began to ache and the family thought it might be from cheerleading practice or that she was experiencing growing pains. After several visits to various doctors to determine what was causing the pain, Hope was diagnosed with a rare form of bone cancer that strikes children between the ages of ten and twenty. When Hope was told about her situation, she didn't let it get her down. There was no doubt in her mind that she was going to overcome the disease and she was absolutely and positively determined that she could.

Although Hope tried chemotherapy, radiation and numerous medications, nothing stopped the cancer from spreading from her legs to her arms, lungs, spine and shoulders. She was, sadly, now in a position that she could request a wish to be granted. This is where Hope's story is unique.

When she was asked what wish she wanted to have, Hope responded with a question to the wish coordinator. She asked, "How many other children are on the wish list in my area?" The response was 155. Hope replied without hesitation, "Then that is what I want. I want to raise enough money to grant all 155 wishes for these kids." This was something that no other child had ever wished for before. When it was explained to Hope that it could take close to a million dollars to fulfill that many wishes, it didn't change her mind. She was even more inspired to do so and convinced that she would be able to reach this enormous, and heartwarming, goal.

Hope's real desire was to have a walk-on part on a television program and be "famous." Her favorite show was *Lizzie McGuire* and her favorite celebrity was Hilary Duff. The wish coordinators thought

Kids With A Cause would be a perfect organization to call and see if Hope's wish to be on television could be fulfilled. The request came to Kids With A Cause during the holiday season and we were not in the office to take the initial call. We were having an unusually busy month and had arranged to visit hospitals each week, conduct toy drives and participate in a food program to help feed the homeless. We did not have enough hours in the day to accommodate every request that we were receiving. I decided to try and fulfill some of the wish requests during the month of January, since December was already full of various holiday activities. This was a decision that still concerns me to this day.

Hope was not aware that the wish organization had contacted me. She was determined that she was going to raise the money to help grant the other kids' wishes and her fundraising efforts began. She started selling silver charms at her school with the simple word "hope" engraved on them. The local wish organization began planning a black-tie "Celebration of Hope" fundraising event and the word about Hope's wish began to spread.

On December 19th, a well-known local newspaper ran a story on Hope that was quickly picked up by nearby radio and television stations. Soon after the initial publication, a few newspapers across the country—looking for an inspirational Christmas article—also printed the story of Hope's unusual and selfless wish. Even the local professional football team convinced the broadcast station to give Hope a few minutes on air to tell her story, which she did. The message of Hope's wish for others was beginning to spread, as was her personal wish to become famous. More and more people were learning about Hope and helping to make her wish come true.

Hope's cancer was not what made her want to help others. Even before her diagnosis, Hope was always helping. She took water bottles to people working at voting booths, she made Easter baskets for homeless children and was always thinking of ways she could help others and cheer them up. Even when she was in her hospital bed with many visitors coming to see her, she would look at them and politely say, "I have sisters and a loving family. There are kids who don't have people with them" and she would encourage her visitors to stop by and visit with some of the other kids in the hospital, too. Hope was always thinking of others.

Whatever our personal beliefs may be, it is not always easy to understand why life has its ups and downs, especially when it comes to the lives of innocent children. Although Hope's health was failing she had the strength to live a few more days and see her dream come closer to reality. One anonymous donor graciously gave $100,000 to help fulfill Hope's dream of granting all 155 wishes for the other children. At this point, she had now not only raised awareness of her wish but she also raised close to $500,000. She still had the one big formal event, scheduled for January 16th, to help her achieve her amazing goal.

When I received the call with the sad news that Hope had passed away on January 4th, I could not hold back the tears. I called Susan and told her all about Hope and her wish. Although I had planned to do what I could for Hope in January, I now knew I didn't respond quickly enough. Susan could tell how upset I was and how much this situation was affecting me and she tried to console me. She reminded me about all the kids we helped in the past and would continue to help in the future and she encouraged me focus on the good we were doing for so many. She was there for me during a painful time, yet I continued to blame myself for not reacting to this request sooner. I vowed that I would never let time or a busy schedule get in the way of helping these precious children and doing what I could to fulfill their undemanding and simple wishes to experience happiness.

Shortly after Hope's passing the wish organization sent me a letter with the following explanation, "Hope constantly talked about her admiration of Hilary. Hope's desire to do this was because she was inspired by Hilary after seeing some sort of charity event that Hilary was involved with." When Hilary learned about Hope and her wish for others we talked about what we could do for Hope's family. We decided to send some gift items from Kids With A Cause to Hope's sisters (who were also Hilary fans) and include a letter to the family from Hilary. In the letter Hilary wrote about what a courageous and strong girl Hope was to not only endure as much as she did at such a young age but also to be so thoughtful and caring of others. Hilary offered her deepest sympathies to Hope's family and friends and expressed her genuine admiration of Hope.

I later found out that the "Celebration of Hope" gala was a big success and that Hope's wish—to fulfill 155 wishes for others—would now come true. Because of her one wish, a five year old boy with a rare blood disorder would now be able to ride a pony; a seven year old girl with Leukemia would be able to go to Disneyland and dance with Cinderella and a fifteen year old with cancer would be able to take a cruise to the Bahamas. The event, in combination with Hope's awareness campaign and fundraising efforts, brought in enough money not only for those three wishes but for the 152 others.

Hope not only achieved her dreams but had both of her wishes come true. She was famous in the eyes of many while helping to fulfill the dreams of others. I keep Hope's charm on my key chain to inspire me everyday and to remember her caring qualities. She is one person, although I never met her, who truly influenced my life and touched my heart.

When Hilary and I would talk about kids and their challenges it wasn't always easy to understand. Why could some kids, like Hilary, be so lucky and others have to experience pain or lose their lives to a terrible disease? Sometimes it just didn't seem fair and Hilary never took anything for granted. She was appreciative of all that life was giving her and continued to work as hard as she could, many times seven days a week, to strive to be her best. Hilary was inspirational to her fans and gave them hope to follow their dreams.

One of Hilary's fans had a big dream—he wanted to go to one of Hilary's concerts, but he lived in a small town that rarely had any type of celebrity event much less a concert arena. This young boy was in good health, lived with his mom and idolized his favorite star. He owned all of Hilary's CDs and memorized the words to her songs. He had hoped, more than anything, that someday he would be able to see her in concert.

As a Christmas surprise, his mom wrapped up the two tickets she had purchased for Hilary's concert. The performance, the closest one to them, would take over *eight hours* to get to by car. She knew how much this meant to her son and she was willing to make the long drive to be with him and watch his dream come true. When Cody opened the present and saw the tickets, he hugged his mom and started thinking about the day he would see his dream girl. It was actually going to happen. Cody held the tickets close to him and couldn't wait to tell all his friends about the best Christmas gift ever.

The concert was scheduled during the winter months and it was in an area with frequent winter blizzards. On the way to the concert the weather was cold and dreary but it was still daylight and Cody and his mom had allowed plenty of time to drive to the concert to enjoy this unbelievable experience together. When they arrived Cody's feet could barely touch the ground. People were everywhere holding "We love you, Hilary" posters and excitement filled the air. When the doors finally opened and the crowds rushed in, Cody and his mom raced to find their seats. They weren't the best seats in the house but Cody was thrilled just to be there—anywhere, as long as he got to see Hilary.

The concert was fantastic, as they all are, because Hilary devotes every ounce of energy she has to give the greatest show she can. She performs almost non-stop with just a few sips of water here and there and words of thanks and appreciation to her fans, in between songs. She rocked the house and Cody was there to see and hear it all. It was hard to think about making that long drive back home but Cody was so excited about the concert that the drive did not seem to be a concern to him or to his mom. They shared a very special time together and it was one evening that Cody didn't want to ever end.

Still several hours from home, the weather conditions started to worsen. The light snow that was falling was now turning into a heavy snowfall and Cody's mom remained in the slow lane because she was not used to driving in snow conditions and it was dark and difficult to see. There were several large trucks on the road that night and one was right behind Cody and his mother. She stepped lightly on her brakes to slow down a bit and the truck behind her decided to pass them. The truck driver misjudged the distance and slightly clipped Cody's mother's car in his attempt to pass, causing the car to spin sideways on the slippery road. As the truck passed their car, the driver realized what happened and stepped on his brakes to slow down. The driver of a second truck was not able to see Cody's mother's car (which was now sitting perpendicular on the road) in time to stop. Cody and his mother were tragically killed in their car that was smashed between the two large trucks on this dreadful winter evening.

The only way I found out about this horrible accident was when I received a phone call from one of the family's relatives. The call was from Cody's aunt and she was crying uncontrollably on the phone when she called our office. She was trying to explain to me what had happened and it was extremely sad to listen to the details of this terrible and tragic situation. I was unsure at the time what made her decide to call Kids With A Cause or what we could possibly do to help during this painful and difficult time.

Cody's aunt was in such a state of shock that, at first, she wasn't sure why she was calling either. She just felt she needed to talk with me, or someone that knew Hilary, about Cody and what had happened. After we spoke for quite a while she finally asked if Hilary could dedicate one of her songs to Cody at her next concert. She thought the family might find comfort in knowing what Hilary respectfully would do in memory of Cody and his mother.

As usual, I called Susan and forwarded the email with the newspaper article about the sad accident. It broke her heart to hear what had happened but she wondered if a song dedication would help the family and ease the pain. She knew the family would not be at the next concert to hear the dedication so she decided to talk with Hilary and find a way they could offer their support to this grieving family.

Hilary decided to dedicate her song *Fly* to Cody and wanted to put a personal message to him on the huge screens behind her during the song. Susan coordinated the necessary arrangements to not only add this message to Hil's show but also to have a photographer there to take pictures of the special dedication. It all happened at lightning speed and the very next night Hilary dedicated her song to Cody. Behind her, for all to see, was Cody's name along with the words, "Dedicated to the memory of a very special fan. You will always be remembered." Susan and I watched Hilary sing *Fly* (which we had seen her perform many times before) and with tears in our eyes we knew that she had never sang it with such emotion as she did that night for Cody.

By the time the concert ended the photo of Hilary singing with the dedication to Cody on the screens behind her was developed, framed and ready for me to ship overnight to the family. I sent it along with a card from Kids With A Cause and hoped that, in some way, this personal dedication from Hilary would bring comfort to the family. When Cody's aunt called to let me know the package arrived, she expressed her deep appreciation and described how overwhelmed the family was with Hilary's concern, response and kindness. I knew that this personal and treasured gift came at a very needed time.

It's not always easy to understand why life unfolds the way it does. Why some people are healthy and strong or rich and famous and others suffer from illness or lose their lives at young ages. Although these mysteries of life are *part* of life, I believe the young children we have lost are smiling on those doing charitable deeds and can actually *see* the pure gold of Hilary's heart.

Chapter 10

A Shining Light For Others

Hilary leads by example and helps promote literacy by reading to a group of young children.

Hilary, always wanting to give to others, was pleased when a corporate sponsor donated teddy bears (dressed in Hilary t-shirts) for her Sweet Sixteen Celebration. These fluffy friends were proudly delivered to disadvantaged youth.

Hilary continued year after year to be a shining light for millions of people throughout the world. It seemed that no matter what she set her mind to do, she did. She worked extremely hard at everything and balanced a very difficult schedule. She spent countless hours in the studio perfecting her music. Her dance rehearsals were vigorous and exhausting. She devoted time to study the scripts for her films and concentrated on how to best portray her character roles. She attended business, marketing and promotional meetings to ensure that her product line would continue to produce quality yet affordable items. She kept her media and publicity commitments for photo shoots, television appearances and film premieres as well as fulfilling ongoing magazine and radio interview requests. She was traveling extensively and keeping up with a very demanding schedule every day.

There were times, of course, when she would be exhausted. Traveling from one side of the globe to the other with drastic time zone changes was not easy. She would lose a day, gain a day and sometimes wondered if it was day or night. But with it all, Hilary didn't complain. She continued to work hard, which took a lot of discipline and sacrifice, to do the best job—no matter what it was—she possibly could. Hilary wanted her devoted fans to know how much their loyalty meant to her. She felt she was fortunate to be in the position she was in and she never took her fans for granted. It was important to her that she did not let them down or disappoint them in any way.

At one point during a delicate balancing act of singing and acting and fashion design, Hilary started to get tired and wasn't feeling too well. She was working 14-16 hour days and wasn't able to get much rest. During this time she was not able to have healthy meals at normal times and knew she needed to take some time, once her projects were finished, to re-energize. Of course the tabloids immediately accused her of an eating disorder when, in fact, she just needed to rest and regain her strength—which she did.

There were also times when, especially as a teenager, she wanted to be with her friends but she had work obligations and would have to pass. Her life was changing the more famous she was becoming and her privacy was not always so private. The days of going to the mall with Haylie or sitting down to enjoy an iced coffee with a friend now often times included the (uninvited) paparazzi. Hilary always tried to remain friendly and outgoing but there were times when she would turn around and drive back home because the paparazzi would be following her and she just needed and wanted some time to herself. Her life was changing even though she still viewed herself as a "regular" person.

Hilary continued to achieve success on many levels and her accomplishments, especially at such a young age, have been amazing. Her ability to remain positive with an optimistic outlook reflected ideal characteristics and her fans looked up to her with great respect. Hilary also set an exceptional example about the importance of working hard and not giving up. She knew that there were many challenges that were not easy to overcome but she was always willing to devote the time it required to achieve her goals.

As the world was looking up to Hilary she continued to project a clean and wholesome image. It was very important to her to emphasize the inner beauty and uniqueness of each individual. She watched as other young celebrities followed popular fashion trends and she felt many of these rising stars were losing their personal identities. She encouraged people to find happiness within and make changes to enhance their health and their life style, not just their physical appearance.

When asked one time by a reporter what she would physically change about herself, she hesitated and then smiled. Although she had areas she wanted to improve she wasn't sure what she wanted to actually *change*. When pressed for an answer she finally blurted out, "I guess my arms", which is not what the reporter was expecting to hear. For most Hollywood stars the automatic answer would have been a long list of cosmetic changes, but Hilary just wanted to have better muscle definition and tone up her arms. She did not look at herself as flawless without need to improve. She was concerned with who she was on the inside and how she treated other people. She felt it was more important to remain true to herself than it was to simply focus on current trends or physical attributes. And she knew that, once again, whatever she wanted to achieve would take persistence and hard work.

She did believe in daily exercise, even if it meant getting up in the early morning hours. She knew that if she didn't take time in the morning to exercise that soon her day would be filled with appointments, meetings and commitments and there would be no time to try and squeeze in a work out. She loved to start her day with Pilates and tried to encourage me to do the same. She once told me, "If you just took twenty minutes for yourself, early in the morning, you would feel the difference the rest of the day." She was pleased with the results she was getting and liked to begin her day feeling good, healthy and focused.

Hilary often referred to herself as just a "regular kid" and in many ways she was. She saw herself as a normal teen, only one that was working in the entertainment industry. She enjoyed the same things as others her age and was experiencing similar teen issues. She was discovering the enjoyment and the heartbreak of boys, friends and relationships. Like any other teenager, the phone was her *lifeline* and she would spend as much time as possible talking to friends when she wasn't working.

People could relate to her because she shared common interests with them. She loved her dogs, her horses and her trampoline. She was an amazing gymnast and loved doing her own stunts. When she was faced with a challenge and doubted her ability, she would stand very still, take a deep breath, concentrate and all of a sudden do a back flip! That was always her test. She knew if she could do that, she was ready to meet the challenge ahead. She had inner strength, confidence and determination to always strive harder at whatever she did.

As Hilary was growing up she continued to be a shining light for others. The more she conveyed her insightful, powerful and positive messages, the more impact and influence she had on people. It was easy to know when Hilary was on the news or in the papers because of the numerous emails, calls and letters I would receive soon after the media coverage. People everywhere were pleased to learn that she did not feel pressure to follow the crowd or pay attention to topics of gossip and they praised her for standing on her own and following her beliefs. She had earned the reputation of being an honest and sincere individual and was living up to it.

Even with her career on the rise she still made time for others. She spent as much time as she could with family and friends. She showed care and concern for those who were sick, hungry or homeless. She opened her heart and continued to show her support to Kids With A Cause and attended special fundraising events. She believed in giving back and was leading the way by her hands-on example and showing others this valuable lesson. Over the years, Hilary touched the lives of millions of people and sometimes I wondered if she was truly aware of her magnetic personality and her tremendous ability to motivate and inspire others.

Because of Hilary's exposure to philanthropy, which began very early in her life, she was able to participate in personally rewarding experiences and ultimately raise awareness of important causes. Her charitable efforts came from her heart and she encouraged others to take an active role and help, too. She took the opportunity, whenever possible, to let people know that it didn't necessarily require "millions and millions of dollars" to make a difference in someone's life and she offered ways for others to lend a helping hand. She reinforced the concept that giving comes from the heart. She knew that simple acts of kindness such as reading to a young child, helping a student with a school project or collecting food for a local food bank were personal ways to help. Her experience taught her that giving was not based solely on financial contributions and she expressed the importance and the impact of humanitarian deeds.

Hilary was changing the way the world viewed charitable giving, especially in the eyes of kids and teens. She was helping others, through her work with Kids With A Cause, and opening doors that encouraged and empowered youth while enriching the lives of children in need. As she continued to lend a helping hand, more and more people were watching and listening. Students began conducting fundraising events such as bake sales, car washes or read-a-thons to contribute to our ongoing programs and services. Many were participating in awareness campaigns such as food drives and clothing collections and extending their support to families in need. People of all ages were finding ways to do their part and lend a helping hand—just like Hilary.

There were also children who wanted to have special "Hilary" birthday parties and celebrate with a *cause*. They did not ask for gifts for themselves but instead they requested that their guests bring something to donate to Kids With A Cause. One day I received a phone call from a parent asking to schedule a time for her and her daughter to drop off some gifts from her daughter's recent birthday party.

The birthday child, who had just turned nine, arrived with her mother at the office with their arms full of gifts. The theme of her party was a Hawaiian luau and she proudly showed me pictures of the bright and colorful party decorations. She had asked her guests to bring one new beach towel and a bottle of bubbles, instead of a gift for her. When the guests arrived they saw several round empty containers (with Hawaiian floral leis and green grass skirts taped around them) that were used for the gift contributions.

The guests were excited to donate their beach towels and bubbles knowing that their gifts would bring a smile to another child. It turned out to be a fun party for all and also one that reinforced giving and helping others. The six containers full of these fabulous items were delivered, with pride, to the Kids With A Cause office. It was clear that this young child felt good about giving these gifts to our charity and said, "I wanted to do something to help kids because of Hilary."

There were others planning special occasions and they, too, wanted to do something to help kids who were less fortunate. One bar mitzvah celebration had beautifully wrapped gift baskets full of toys that were used as centerpieces. Next to each basket was a note about Kids With A Cause and a heartfelt explanation that these special gifts were going to be delivered to a child in a hospital.

Another young student had a pizza and movie night at her house and collected donations as admission. Lemonade stands were popping up across the country and a brother and sister worked together to clean out their closets and have a garage sale to benefit Kids With A Cause. In almost every situation, it was Hilary that was inspiring these young philanthropists. Her message of "everyone can help" was proving to be true.

Kids were sending emails and letters to our office telling us about what they were doing to help others. Packages would arrive with thoughtful notes from kids who were motivated by Hilary to make a difference. One box full of goodies included a letter from a young girl explaining, "All of these things are for the kids that need them. I went to Hilary Duff's website and found your foundation and I decided to check it out. I printed the page that I found and showed it to my mom. I wanted to help out the people that needed these things. So I put flyers up at schools and businesses and we ended up with all these things. I hope you like all these things and I hope they're acceptable." The letter was signed by a nine-year-old girl as, "Somebody who cares."

As more and more people were becoming aware of Hilary's heart there were also more and more requests for her support. People knew she was a member of Kids With A Cause and reached out to us for assistance. There were ideas about products, promotions, fundraising events and more. I created "Hilary files" for the office and discussed each opportunity with Susan. Although it was impossible to fulfill them all, careful thought was given to each request. It was important that Hilary's involvement would have a direct benefit, rather than merely adding her name to a program seeking the enhancement of a popular celebrity.

It was not only Hilary's care and concern for others but also the manner in which she conducted herself that made her a shining star. She was raised *southern-style* and knew good manners. She behaved in a polite and dignified manner and yet had the fun spirit of a kid. She had her career responsibilities but she also had her day-to-day chores like most *regular* kids. She fed the dogs, made her bed, cleaned her room and did what was expected of her. At least most of the time.

There was one time when Hilary had a day off and her friends called and wanted to get together with her. When she asked her mom if she could go with them, Susan said she could as long as her room was cleaned. With little time before she was supposed to meet her friends, Hilary decided it would be faster if she just pushed her shoes under her bed and spent time hanging up clothes and straightening things up. When the room was clean, Susan went in and was ready to compliment Hilary on a job well done when she noticed the tip of one shoe peeking out from under the bed. She pointed to the shoe and questioned Hilary about it and Hilary knew that the job was not completed, at least not to mom's satisfaction. Hilary pulled the shoes out from under the bed and put them away in their proper place in her closet. Susan simply said, "You see, Hilary, that wasn't so hard to do, was it? Now you can go" and Hilary gave her a big kiss as she hurried out the door.

Anyone who knew the Duffs knew that their parenting skills were a big reason that Hilary was able to stay grounded and could relate so well to other kids. In many ways, Hilary's life at home was much like anyone else her age. There were responsibilities, expectations and there were also consequences. Hilary and Haylie knew the rules and were not excused because of their busy schedules or career obligations.

Truth, honesty, dignity and respect were important core values introduced early in Haylie and Hilary's lives. Even as they gained an enormous amount of fame and publicity, the Duffs were not pretentious people. There were many times when I would help arrange the logistics for a charity-related event and would be asked about the type of vehicle the Duffs required. Would it be a stretch limo? Did they have a specific car they preferred? It was always a surprise when I would tell the transportation company that the Duffs preferred to ride in a van and they would pass on the offer of a limo.

Stardom was not what was filling Hilary's heart but learning about all the kids who were doing things to make a difference, because of *her influence*, truly touched her. She felt fortunate to be in a position that she was able to have a positive impact on others. If she could deliver messages of care, concern, compassion and hope that could help enrich the lives of children everywhere—then that's what she would continue to do.

Hilary's strong work ethics, her commitment to her responsibilities, her respect and concern for others combined with her positive attitude and bright outlook continue to inspire people everywhere. She is a unique individual who represents a shining light for others that only gets brighter with each passing day.

Chapter 11

Where Did She Go Right?

As Hilary continued to balance a busy schedule, she always made time to bring happiness to others.

Making a Difference

Hilary has made a difference to millions of people, including me, and I am lucky to know her and call her my friend.

♥

The title to one of Hilary's songs, *Where Did I Go Right?* echoes why she stands apart from others and why she is such a powerful and influential role model for millions of people around the world. She looks at life in a positive way and accepts mistakes as learning experiences. She has common sense and realizes she is not perfect and won't always make the right or best decision. She also knows that part of growing up is accepting challenges and risks along with potential consequences that may follow.

So where did this little girl from Texas, without extensive acting experience as a young child, go right? Hilary would tell you that there were many lessons in life she learned by watching, listening, trying and not giving up. Her determination was unwavering and often times she viewed obstacles as opportunities and she "went right" in many ways.

One way, that also helped her meet the challenges ahead, was her willingness to explore new horizons and experience new situations. She was eager to try the unknown, including moving to Los Angeles. It could have been overwhelming for her to leave her ranch-style life in Texas and move to a fast paced big city located in the heart of the entertainment industry. But instead of feeling overwhelmed or intimidated, Hilary was excited and ready for the challenge. She arrived with an open mind and began to adjust comfortably to the new and exciting environment. The valuable lessons she was about to learn would not be forgotten. Her experiences would provide her with the skills and knowledge she would need for her future success.

She also “went right” by learning and understanding the importance of healthy eating habits and reducing her consumption of fast foods and soft drinks. Hilary did many of the same, and normal, things that other kids did. She liked to play video games, listen to music, hang out with her friends, talk on the phone and eat her favorite foods. When Hilary was a young teen she loved to eat hamburgers and French fries and drink Dr. Pepper. She also liked candy and desserts, just like many of the friends her age. She did not change her eating habits over night and, as a young teenager, she was sometimes reluctant to try new foods.

One time she was having dinner at a restaurant with a group of people including her music manager and her mom. When someone at the table decided to order sushi, Hilary could not believe that “raw fish could actually taste good” and made faces and sounds of disgust with the thought of eating fish that had not been cooked. Her music manager asked if she had ever tried sushi and her reply was simply, “No.” He then gave her the standard adult response, “Well, Hilary, if you haven’t tried it, how do you know you don’t like it?” He convinced her to try at least one item and he suggested vegetable tempura or a California roll to let her ease into this new food adventure. She agreed and ordered a California roll. Surprisingly, she liked it. She then experimented each time with something new and discovered that she absolutely loved sushi. There were many times when she was working that it would not be unusual to find a platter of sushi waiting for her in the refrigerator in her production trailer.

The burgers and fries were in her past and she was now enjoying a variety of healthy foods. As she explored many new tastes her eating habits slowly began to change and now included several healthy and nutritious items. Today, Hilary is very conscious of what she eats and reads the ingredients label on almost everything she buys. She still enjoys some of her old favorites occasionally, including hamburgers and desserts, but she doesn't include them as part of her daily diet.

As she was getting older there was also a lot of pressure (particularly on young celebrities in the public eye) to be thin, but Hilary felt it was just as important to be healthy and *feel* good, as it was to *look* good. With healthy eating habits and daily exercise she was able to reduce inches where she wanted and firm and tone her muscles. She was pleased to see and feel the results and she now realized how important it was to make good food choices and devote time to exercise. She was happy with her healthy life style and pleased to take steps that she felt were right for her.

Another important area where Hilary "went right" was her determination to be herself. She purposely decided not to follow fashion trends that she felt were too revealing for her age or did not suit her well. She had the ability and talent to create her own unique look and she felt comfortable with who she was both inside and out. I found it very refreshing to see so many young fans that looked up to Hilary and admired her for her remarkable qualities, not simply for what she was wearing.

There were times that she would wonder where she "went right" and question why she was so lucky. She never took her success for granted. She was always appreciative of her fans and the people around her that helped her take critical steps in her career. Hilary showed respect to others and treated people with the same respect that she would want in return. Differences of opinion did not develop into arguments but rather discussions. Hilary was respectful of the knowledge and expertise of those involved in her various business facets, mostly adults, and she strived to listen and learn, respect their opinions and reach productive solutions.

As a teenager growing up in the world of entertainment, there may have been times that Hilary felt she knew what was best for her. She might have wanted to act on one of her ideas without seeking input from the business professionals around her. She knew, however, that it would be best to work with these experienced individuals who had proven track records of success and learn from them.

Hilary "went right" by respecting and appreciating the unique talents of the individuals on her team and she made decisions after she had a clear understanding of their views. This was not always easy because it involved trust—which is not usually the first word that comes to mind when one thinks of those involved in the entertainment business. Many people view industry personnel as competitive and greedy individuals who care only about what will end up in their own pockets, rather than what is best for the artist or actor. Susan knew, and Hilary learned, how to "run with the big guys" and make the right decisions. They did not respond to pressure tactics or agree to do something without careful thought first.

Courage is another way that Hilary "went right." Many people say they want to do something, but *talk* or *wishful thinking* is all it turns out to be. Hilary is a girl of her word and a girl of action. There were many times she had to take courageous steps to earn her fame and sustain her popularity. The public was not necessarily aware of some of Hilary's courageous moments because she always performed as a professional, even when confronting a difficult situation. On various occasions I observed Hilary's ability to put tough situations aside and focus strictly on her work without any apparent distractions.

One very difficult moment for her was the day Little Dog passed away. Little had been part of Hilary's life since she was four years old. While living on their ranch in Texas, Hilary was playing outside one day when she saw this very small dog walking up the long entrance road and heading towards her. The dog was a young pup that was thin, undernourished and all alone. It was hard to believe this tiny animal had walked such a distance and it was a mystery as to how Little Dog found the road to the Duffs' ranch in the first place.

When Hilary saw the dog getting closer she excitedly called to her mom in the house, "Mommy, mommy—come and look." Susan glanced out the window and then went outside to see what Hilary was so excited about and picked up the weak little puppy. Hilary asked, “Can we keep him?” which was immediately followed by her intense curiosity as she questioned, “What *is* it?” The dog was extremely small and Susan replied, “It’s a little dog, Hilary, but it doesn’t belong to us.” Susan knew the right thing to do was to try and find the owner. She took the little dog, Haylie and Hilary and went into town to put up posters about the lost dog in an attempt to locate the owner.

As week by week went by there were no calls regarding the dog and the Duffs continued to feed and care for the little pup until the owner showed up. With each passing day, the little dog became more and more like a new member of the family and Haylie and Hilary were thrilled. Finally, after no communication from anyone about the lost dog, the Duffs decided it would be best to keep her and give her the love and affection she needed. When it came to naming her, the only name the Duff family had ever called her was “Little Dog” so that became her permanent identity.

Little was a *big* part of Hilary’s life. As Hilary grew up, so did Little. Hilary took her small companion with her everywhere she went. She taught her tricks that Little would only do for Hilary. She traveled with her and took her on tour whenever she could. She even had Little ride in a parade with her. Hilary realized Little Dog was getting older and before long new dogs were added to the Duff household to give Little companionship and help keep her as playful and active as possible.

On the morning of Hilary's concert in San Diego, Susan and the girls woke up early to prepare for their long drive to the venue. It was on that morning that Hilary, sadly, found Little Dog passed away. The family was very upset yet they knew that Little Dog had lived a full life and they took comfort in knowing they had given her a loving home for several years.

When I saw Hilary that day she was as kind as always to her fans and her Kids With A Cause guests and greeted them with her warm, beautiful smile. When Susan told me that they had lost Little Dog that morning, it was hard to believe that Hilary was able to perform with the same energy and enthusiasm as always. She knew her fans came to see her and she refused to let them down in spite of the loss and sadness she was feeling. No one knew the ache in her heart and her performance was spectacular, as always.

Her integrity was another way that Hilary "went right." No matter what project she worked on from her fashion line to her own perfume fragrance to the lyrics of her songs, Hilary did not take short cuts to produce inferior products. It was worth her time and effort to make sure that everything with her name attached reflected quality and adhered to her high standards of professionalism. She worked on her own timeline that produced the right results instead of rushing to release her products to meet market trends. Hilary had the integrity to do the right thing at the right time.

Hilary's ability to follow her heart and do what was right also helped her rise above the tabloid news about her. There were a few times in the early years of her career that she would become upset when she would learn of an untrue article printed about her or find out about a statement she never made or hear of a false rumor she supposedly started. Even though she knew the truth she wished the public knew the truth, too. She didn't feel she had to defend herself on these issues because the truth was in her heart. She soon realized, however, that everything written or said about her was part of the price she was going to have to pay as her celebrity status grew.

Hilary was being watched by millions of people around the world and they wanted to learn as much as they could about this popular teen. The press was eager to publish anything they could including stories about her personal relationships and private family matters. When she began dating it was not a quiet innocent romance—once it became worldwide news. As much as she would politely respond to press questions and avoid personal details, her private life still ended up public. There were times she actually found it interesting, and sometimes funny, to read about someone she was supposedly dating or about relationships with people she had never even met.

Although it was upsetting for Hilary to hear or read some of the unkind (and untrue) negative comments about members of her family, she knew that the people in her life who were close to her were aware of the truth. It bothered her, especially when the comments were about her mom, to think that people may actually believe these heartless statements to be true. Susan always tried to do what was best for the girls and often times was criticized for decisions she made on their behalf. She was always more concerned about their health and safety than she was about a financial gain or publicity opportunity.

The interesting part, and I think unfortunate, is that Hilary's charitable efforts rarely, if ever, were included in the media. Although *I* knew the tremendous joy she was bringing to children, and *she* knew, and the *thousands of kids* she was helping knew, the general public did not. It seemed that charity work just didn't have the sizzle the tabloids wanted to feature and Hilary's good deeds were not frequently known or publicized. She learned, in time, not to concern herself with what others heard about her or what they read about her and chose instead to ignore the gossip and stay focused on her career and the importance of giving back. She continued to work hard, stay true to herself and her fans, and try her best at everything she did.

Hilary also "went right" because she was willing to accept the responsibilities that came along with her commitments. There were many mornings that she did not have the luxury of sleeping in and starting her day in a leisurely fashion because of her obligations. Hilary knew it was her responsibility to keep her word and follow through on her commitments whether it involved a band rehearsal, a photo shoot, phone calls or meetings. She was not a person who would create excuses or offer vague explanations in an attempt to reschedule something she had promised to do. She would wake up, get up and do whatever needed to be done.

Were there times when she wanted to take a day off and just relax—of course there were, but Hilary knew that her work, her responsibilities and her commitments came first. She was motivated to succeed and was willing to put in the time required to ensure her work, no matter what she was doing and what it entailed, always reflected her best.

Hilary made many good decisions and it was clear where she "went right." Her curiosity and willingness to learn, combined with her drive and determination, helped her achieve successful results in the many diverse aspects of her career. She was able to recognize important qualities and live her life by them. She knew she needed to make the sometimes-difficult decisions and take the sometimes-challenging steps that would enable her to be a person that lived by the characteristics and qualities that she valued.

Chapter 12

Her Heart Is Bigger Than Her Fame

Happy Birthday, Hilary!
Thank you for all the beautiful memories.
May we share many more in the future.

♥

Dear Readers,

As you begin this last chapter of *Hilary's Heart,* I share with you the letter that I wrote to Hilary on her 21st birthday. It is my hope that now you know and understand the qualities that make Hilary an exceptional person with a compassionate heart. It is also my intention to encourage you and help you realize that you, too, can make a difference. I ask that you remember to think of others and do what you can to lend a helping hand whenever and wherever possible. I strongly believe that if everyone did *one kind thing every day of their lives,* the world would be a better place for all.

Thank you for taking the time to read; now it's the time to act.

Dear Hilary,

I am writing this to you on your 21st Birthday, September 28, 2008.

The world was blessed when you were born. There is no one else like you and never will be. Your mom told me that when she first looked at you, there was a "greatness" about you. Although she couldn't tell exactly what it was, she was sure that you would do something special with your life. And that you have. Because of your caring qualities and loving heart, less fortunate children around the world have smiled and felt joy. They have been given hope because of you.

Being charitable is not an obligation; it's a choice. You decided to lend a helping hand to children in need because you cared and wanted to make a difference in their lives. Your work with Kids With A Cause has been, without a doubt, the single most important factor that facilitated our ability to help children in need around the world. I feel extremely fortunate that you always kept Kids With A Cause in your heart and continued to help us, help kids.

I believe we each have a purpose in life and a direction to follow on our unique and personal journey. Although it may not be apparent to us or easy to recognize the gifts we've been given, I often felt that your warmth, generosity and genuine concern for others were precious gifts you eagerly shared with so many. It seemed as though you were a beautiful little angel going through life touching the hearts of everyone around you. There were times when I wondered if you truly realized the tremendous impact you were making on each and every person's life. I know that I am one of the fortunate people whose heart you touched and I thank you for being an angel in my life. You have given me wonderful memories that will never be forgotten.

When trying to decide what to get you or what to do for your 21st birthday, I realized that there was only one gift I could give you that no one else could—a gift from my heart. I decided to write a book sharing the beautiful memories I have of you growing up. You might not read this book from beginning to end but I hope that your children (and even your grandchildren) will have the opportunity to learn more about you as a child and understand the "greatness" you gave to the world's children.

This book was written as a tribute to you and an everlasting gift of giving. It is my hope that the remarkable story of your heart will motivate and inspire others. Your contribution to the children of the world and your desire to enhance their lives is a story that will never be forgotten. The legacy of your charitable work will continue from one generation to the next and *Hilary's Heart* will help assist children who need our support and deserve our affection.

I know there were times that it wasn't always easy for you with the demanding schedule you had, but every kind gesture you extended to me and to Kids With A Cause never went unnoticed. I don't know if I could ever put into words how much you mean to me or if I could ever truly thank you for all that you have done for the children whose lives you've changed. You have grown from a caring child to a dignified young lady that I truly admire and deeply respect.

You have been a bright light to so many children. Your generosity and loving heart helped orphan children in Mexico, India, Fiji and South Africa. You also offered support for the young survivors of Hurricane Katrina, the Asian tsunami, the California wildfires, the Galveston floods, the Greensburg tornado and several other emergency situations our charity responded to in many places around the world.

In our own country, children across the nation have benefited from your kindness. You helped create memories that will last a lifetime for children who have had very little to hold on to during difficult times. These children, as all children, deserve to have a roof over their head, food to eat, a warm bed to sleep in and individuals who will protect, nurture, guide and love them. Sadly, this is not the case for all children and many are abandoned, neglected or abused. Others face medical challenges or live in poverty. No matter what situation these innocent children have had to face, you have always been there for them.

You took time to visit with children and teens in hospitals and cheer them up. You made wishes come true for children facing life-threatening illnesses. You offered encouragement and support to those who were victims of natural disasters. You gave food to the hungry and provided educational support for the poor. You inspired those who were weak to be strong and you did it all without any expectation in return. You gave personally, from your heart, to me and to Kids With A Cause and that is what this book, *Hilary's Heart*, captures. It's not a story about a hero, although many view you that way. It's a book about a young humanitarian —*you*— who cares and encourages everyone to do something to help others.

I don't have many regrets in my life or past experiences I'd like to change, although I do wish that you could have been with me more often to see what a difference you were making to these precious children. How I wish you could have seen the reactions when I gave your fashion clothing to children who idolized you. They would scream, squeal, giggle and jump up and down when they received their *Stuff by Hilary Duff* jeans or t-shirt or skirt or jacket. They would hold the item up close to their heart, squeeze it and smile from ear to ear. These kids love you and even though many of them live thousands of miles away, these gifts helped them feel a special closeness to you and gave them some desperately needed comfort.

I wonder what my life would have been like without you. Whether you know it or not, you have been a shining star for me, too. Knowing your schedule and all that you were committed to do, I can honestly say I don't know any adults, much less kids or teens, that could have kept up with you. You sacrificed a lot and even with hectic day-to-day activities and commitments, you continued to do whatever you could to help out.

You are a beacon of light that projects hope for a brighter tomorrow. You represent the good in the world and your enthusiasm is contagious. Your ability to maintain a positive attitude and your determined outlook on life are inspiring examples for young people, and everyone, to follow.

I will always remember the many laughs we shared (like the time you put my dog, Homer, on the trampoline with you and giggled as you jumped higher and higher causing him to bounce up and down, too) and the memorable moments we shared (like capturing our private moment to meet Nelson

Mandela together at the UN). You have given me wonderful memories that I will hold in my heart forever. Even with your incredible talents and abilities, I believe that your *heart* is bigger than your *fame*.

It has been a joy watching you grow up and I am pleased to say that whenever I am asked if I know Hilary Duff, I can say with certainty and pride, "Yes, and I am honored that I do."

I thank you for being—*you.* When your mom saw "greatness" in you, I know now that what she saw was your heart. At one time you wrote to me, "Thank you for showing me a better way" and I feel now that I should return the compliment to you! I will always have a special place in my heart for you and will cherish the years we have known each other.

As you turn 21 today, I think about how interesting it will be to see what the future will bring and where your journey in life will take you. No matter what the future holds, I know with you starring in it—it will be fantastic.

I send you my love and I wish you health, happiness and everything you truly deserve today and everyday throughout your life. May you receive the blessings that you have so generously given to others.

All My Love Always,

Linda

Acknowledgments

A heartfelt thanks to Hilary and the entire Duff family for all the wonderful memories

The author also wishes to thank the following for their encouragement, support and assistance:

Rand Baker, Bernadette Beglin, Andy Biglin, Marty Jagodnik, Rod Jones, Diana Tucker and Carol Winokur

Graphic Designers
Teresa May-Strootmann and Jessie Seely

Cover Design
Teresa May-Strootmann

And special thanks to the children and families who opened their hearts and shared their stories.

Photo Credits

The publisher acknowledges with thanks the following sources of photographs:

Front Cover
Buena Vista Records/Hollywood Records

Chapter 1
TOP: TM Harvey Comics, Inc.
BOTTOM: Twentieth Century Fox Home Entertainment

Chapter 2
TOP: Provided by author
BOTTOM: Provided by author

Chapter 3
TOP: Park Lane School
BOTTOM: Provided by author

Chapter 4
TOP: Provided by author
BOTTOM: The Strawberry Festival Association

Chapter 5
TOP: Kurtis Young
BOTTOM: City News

Chapter 6
TOP: Anthony Cutajar/Popstar!
BOTTOM: Provided by author

LIZZIE MCGUIRE PHOTO: The Disney Channel ©Disney
CADET KELLY PHOTO: The Disney Channel ©Disney
TEEN MAGAZINE COVER: James Allen

Chapter 7
TOP: *Lizzie McGuire* Wardrobe Department
BOTTOM: Mark Sullivan

Chapter 8
TOP: Anthony Cutajar/Popstar!
BOTTOM: Anthony Cutajar/Popstar!

Chapter 9
TOP: Provided by author
BOTTOM: Louise Kinross

Chapter 10
TOP: Hospital for Sick Children
BOTTOM: Anthony Cutajar/Popstar!

Chapter 11
TOP: Dreams Come True
BOTTOM: Linda Soloman

Chapter 12
Anthony Cutajar/Popstar!

Back Cover
Tracey Seaborn

All autographed headshots, DVDs, magazine covers and publicity photos were given to author by Hilary Duff.

About The Author

Linda Finnegan, a native Southern Californian, began her career at eleven years old when she created a babysitting service (with mom nearby to assist if needed). It was obvious to everyone around her that, even at this young age, she had a tremendous passion for young children and the ability to positively impact their lives.

Her career path since then has taken her many directions but her unwavering devotion to children has never changed. Linda has dedicated her life to educating, enriching and improving the lives of children everywhere. Before she began her work in philanthropy, Linda taught over 700 preschool children, wrote educational curriculum, directed summer camps, served as director of a preschool franchise, wrote, produced and appeared in children's educational programs and wrote and directed children's academic and theatrical workshops.

Linda's first step in the non-profit world was her position as Executive Director of the Audrey Hepburn Children's Fund in Los Angeles, California. Linda's ability to inspire and motivate people, particularly kids, served as valuable assets when she founded her own non-profit organization, Kids With A Cause, in 1999.

Linda is all about *heart.* She is a woman with passion, desire, drive, determination and ambition to change the world for children. It is Linda's intent to give you an insight to Hilary Duff's heart through her memories in this book. As Linda would say to you, "If each of you who reads *Hilary's Heart* thinks about Hilary and lends a helping hand to someone, then you have captured the spirit of the personal and heartfelt gift of giving— just like Hilary."

www.ingramcontent.com/pod-product-compliance
Ingram Content Group UK Ltd.
Pitfield, Milton Keynes, MK11 3LW, UK
UKHW040602210726
13854UKWH00008B/1808